The Little English Handbook for Canadians

Second Edition

James B. Bell

Edward P. J. Corbett

1807 1982

John Wiley & Sons Canada Limited
Toronto

Canadian Cataloguing in Publication Data

Bell, James B., 1921–
   The little English handbook for Canadians
Includes index.
ISBN 0-471-79894-0 (bound)
ISBN 0-471-79892-4 (pbk)
1. English language—Rhetoric.   I. Corbett, Edward P.J.   II. Title.
PE1408.B245 1981 808'.042   C81-094896-6

Printed and bound in Canada by Tri-Graphic Printing (Ottawa) Limited
   12   13   14   15

PROOFREADERS' MARKS

⌒	close up space
ℐ	delete
ℐ (circled)	delete and close up space
#	separate with a space
∧	insert here what is indicated in the margin
¶	start new paragraph
no ¶	no paragraph; run in with previous paragraph
⊙/	insert period
∧/	insert comma
;/	insert semicolon
:/	insert colon
⊢M⊣/	insert em dash
⊢M⊣/⊢M⊣	insert pair of em dashes
=/	insert hyphen
⌄/	insert apostrophe
(*cap.*)	use capital letter here
(*lc*)	use lowercase letter here
(*ital*)	set in italic type
(*rom*)	set in roman type
(*sc*)	set in small capitals
(*bf*)	set in boldface type
(*tr*)	transpose letters or words

Preface

This handbook is designed to serve as a guide on basic matters of grammar, style, paragraphing, punctuation, and mechanics for those engaged in writing public prose. By "public prose" is meant that dialect of written English most commonly used in the newspapers, magazines, and books that the majority of educated native speakers read. This ranges in style from the formal to the casual, from the literary to the colloquial. But because public prose seeks to be intelligible to a general audience, it avoids the strictly in-group vocabulary of various professional, regional, and social groups, and it observes the rules of grammar as taught in the schools.

The use of this term is not intended to disparage the other current dialects, most of which serve well the needs of some of the people all of the time and all of the people some of the time. Obviously, spoken English, with its own wide range of professional, regional, and social dialects, serves the needs of more people more often than written English does. In fact, many people speak more words in a single week than they will write during a lifetime. When linguists say that the spoken language is the primary language, they mean

The Little English Handbook

that the spoken language comes first in point of time (centuries before the written form developed) and use (in a single lifetime, before the written language is learned). Also, more natives have a command of the spoken language than have a command of both the spoken and the written. However, despite the primacy of the spoken language, there are occasions when many, if not most, native speakers must use the written language in order to record or communicate their thoughts, needs, and feelings. It is for those occasions that this handbook is designed.

When people wish to communicate in the written medium, it is natural for them to resort—or wish that they could resort—to a more sophisticated style of language than the one they are accustomed to using in the conduct of their everyday affairs. Actually, in their first fumbling efforts at writing, they might succeed better if they used the lexical and syntactical resources acquired from daily practice in the oral medium. But, as the written transcription of impromptu talk reveals, the spoken language is often marked by redundancy of language, imprecision of diction, and loose, rambling, dislocated sentence patterns. Words and structures that may have communicated adequately in the oral medium because of the aid furnished by voice and gesture are something less than adequate when inscribed on paper. For effective written communication, words must be more precise, structures tighter, and organization more discernible; and graphic devices of punctuation and mechanics must be relied on to do what the intonation of the voice does in the oral medium. The kind of public prose used by newscasters on television and radio and by writers in newspapers, magazines, and books has proven to be the most efficient medium for communicating on paper with a general audience.

Preface

This little handbook deals with those matters of grammar, style, paragraphing, punctuation, and mechanics that we know to be the most common and persistent problems in the expressive part of the writing process. For answers to the larger or more subtle problems in writing prose, you will have to consult one of the comprehensive rhetoric handbooks that are readily available. We do not, for instance, provide guidance in all the uses of the comma; some of these are never or seldom a problem for writers. Instead, we deal only with those half-dozen conventions of the comma that are most often ignored or misused and that are most crucial for the preservation of clarity. If you master these six, you can rest assured that there are no really serious mistakes that you can make in the use (or omission) of the comma.

Some of the principles governing the system of writing have been established by convention; others represent a recommendation from a number of available options. Accordingly, in most cases, **we have stated the guiding principle in definite, unequivocal terms.** It should quickly be added, however, that there are no absolute prescriptions in matters of language. Where choices are available, a selection must be guided by a consideration of the subject matter, occasion, desired effect, and audience. But in our experience, the people who need the guidance of a handbook like this want simple, straightforward answers to their queries e.g., **"How do I punctuate this compound sentence?"** They will be helped very little by advice such as, "In most cases, you should separate the two clauses of a compound sentence with a comma, but often when the clauses are short, you can dispense with the comma without any loss of clarity." Such writers will be helped more if they are told that they should *always* put a comma in front of the

The Little English Handbook

coordinating conjunction that joins the two independent clauses of a compound sentence. There is also a practical value attaching to the unequivocal advice: rarely will writers go wrong if they follow it, but they may expect to go wrong rather frequently if they ignore it.

It is assumed that users of this handbook have acquired at least a basic knowledge of formal grammar and that the grammatical system to which they have most likely been exposed is the "traditional" one. Thus when such terms as *compound sentence, independent clause,* and *participial phrase* are used, writers will probably be able to recognize the structures to which the terms refer. Also, the diagram of structures that accompanies many of the statements of principle will serve as a visual aid for those whose knowledge of traditional terminology has faded and for those whose training has been predominantly in structural grammar or in transformational-generative grammar. Thus, the "picture" of a structure will usually be a sufficient guide for those who are impatient with, or are baffled by, technical terminology. However, to ensure maximum comprehension, we have furnished the book with a glossary of grammatical terms.

By concentrating on matters of grammar, style, paragraphing, punctuation, and mechanics, we do not wish to imply that these are the most important concerns of "good writing." We do believe, however, that observance of these "basics" will help writers to improve the accuracy and clarity of their written communications.

James B. Bell
Edward P. J. Corbett

Preface to the Second Edition

In response to comments and suggestions made by teachers and students, we have made a few changes to this second edition of *The Little English Handbook for Canadians*. The general plan of the handbook remains the same, however, and the same clear presentation of text and examples has been retained.

The section on letter writing has been updated and augmented to include new trends in letter format, instructions for set-up of different letter styles, and diagrammatic representations of letter parts and styles.

The material on paragraph development has been expanded to include advice on specific methods of developing a paragraph.

In response to teachers' requests, a Glossary of Usage has been added. Although the list must not be regarded as exhaustive, the usage errors dealt with are those that occur most frequently in student writing.

The Modern Language Association (MLA) system of documentation which was included in the first edition satisfied the demands of students and teachers of the humanities. To meet the needs of the social sciences, the system of documenting a research paper prescribed by the American Psychological Association (APA) has been included in this edition.

The Little English Handbook

All these additions have been incorporated into the same practical format that made the first edition popular. It is our hope that this will serve to make the second edition even more useful as a reference and classroom tool.

James B. Bell
Edward P. J. Corbett

Acknowledgements

I wish to acknowledge the criticisms and suggestions provided by colleagues at the University of Alberta: Dr. G. Prideaux, Chairman, Department of Linguistics; Dr. G. Moyles, Department of English; Dr. G. Farmer and Dr. S. Ubelacker, Department of Secondary Education. I am indebted to James MacInnis, Victoria Composite High School, for his advice on materials proposed for inclusion in the text. To the many teachers who commented on the suitability of particular parts of the book, I express my gratitude. I owe a special debt to Miss Adell Nyberg, graduate student at the University of Alberta, who assisted so capably and who provided a constant flow of optimism and enthusiasm.

Finally I wish to thank the production and editorial staff, especially Mary Macchiusi and Dee Pennock. To Kathryn Dean for her meticulous editing and helpful suggestions, I express my gratitude.

James B. Bell
Faculty of Education
University of Alberta

Note to the Writer

You are fortunate if you have an instructor or an editor or a knowledgeable friend who will read what you have written and call attention to the strengths and weaknesses of your prose by writing comments in the margin or at the end of your paper. Comments of that sort, especially when they are judicious and constructive, can be of great help to you in improving your writing. You should value those personal notes, and whenever the correction, question, suggestion, praise, or blame in them strikes you as being well grounded, you would do well to heed it.

To call attention, however, to routine matters of grammar, paragraphing, punctuation, or mechanics, your accommodating critic may resort to some kind of shorthand notations. If your critic knows that you have a copy of this handbook, he or she may underline or encircle something in your manuscript and write a number in the margin. If, for instance, your critic scribbles the number **49** in the margin, you know that you should look at item **49** in the section on mechanics. Turning to this item in the handbook, you will find that it has to do with italicizing certain kinds of titles. Perhaps you failed to italicize the title of a book you mentioned, or perhaps instead of italicizing the title of the book, you enclosed it in

The Little English Handbook

quotation marks. The principle stated opposite the number **49** may be all that you need to read. But if you need further enlightenment about what you have done wrong, you can look at the graphic diagram of the structure involved (if one is presented for that principle) or at the examples printed below the principle, or you can go on to read the explanation of the principle.

For more complicated matters, the explanation in the handbook may not be sufficient to point out what you have done wrong, or to prevent you from making the mistake again. If so, you should arrange to have a conference with the critic of your prose. Although the correction symbols in the margin may strike you as being heartlessly impersonal, it would be a mistake for you to regard them as peevish slaps on the wrist. They are intended to help you discover how to put your written prose in the "proper" form.

This handbook is also intended to serve as a guide to writers who do not have instructors or friends to read and criticize what they have written. If kept at hand, along with such other reference books as a dictionary and a thesaurus, this handbook can be a useful guide for writers when they sit down to write something that they want others to read. The reference charts on the endpages will direct them to the section that deals with the particular problem of the moment. For example, "Should the modifying clause in this sentence be enclosed with commas?" Somewhere in its pages, the handbook provides a straightforward answer to that query.

Contents

Contents

Punctuation 34 –45

Mechanics 45 – 56

Contents

Format of the Research Paper

Formats for Letters

Legend

Some of the principles developed in this handbook are illustrated with graphic models.

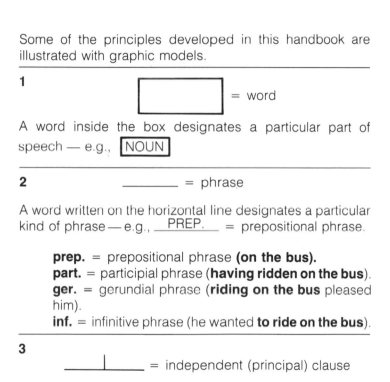

1

☐ = word

A word inside the box designates a particular part of speech — e.g., [NOUN]

2

_____ = phrase

A word written on the horizontal line designates a particular kind of phrase — e.g., __PREP.__ = prepositional phrase.

> **prep.** = prepositional phrase **(on the bus).**
> **part.** = participial phrase (**having ridden on the bus**).
> **ger.** = gerundial phrase (**riding on the bus** pleased him).
> **inf.** = infinitive phrase (he wanted **to ride on the bus**).

3

____|____ = independent (principal) clause

An independent clause, sometimes referred to as a principal clause, can stand by itself as a grammatically complete sentence — e.g., **He rode on the bus.**

Legend

The vertical line is used to separate the subject and predicate in a clause.

4

 = dependent (subordinate) clause

A dependent (subordinate) clause cannot stand by itself as a grammatically complete sentence. The following abbreviation printed on the platform of the first vertical line (T) designates a particular kind of dependent (subordinate) clause — e.g., adv.

adv.
⊤___|___ = dependent (subordinate) adverb clause.

= noun clause (He claimed **that he rode on the bus**).

adj. = adjective clause (The man **who rode on the bus** was pleased).

adv. = adverb clause (He was late **because he rode on the bus**).

Two symbols (✔) and (**X**) are used to indicate correct and incorrect sentences respectively.

5 ✔ = correct or improved sentence — e.g., Tom and Bill ride on the bus.

6 **X** = incorrect or poorly constructed sentence — e.g., Tom and Bill rides on the bus.

Format of Manuscript

In preparing the final draft of a manuscript, follow the specific directions about format given by your instructor or editor. However, if no specific directions are given, you can be confident that the format of your manuscript will be acceptable if you observe the following conventions:

1

Write on one side of the paper only.

2

Double-space the lines of prose, whether you handwrite or typewrite.

A manuscript submitted to an editor for consideration must be typewritten and double-spaced.

3

Preserve a left-hand and a right-hand margin.

On the left-hand side, leave a 3-4 cm margin. On the right-hand side, try to preserve about a 2 or 3 cm margin. If you are handwriting your manuscript on theme paper, the vertical red line will set your left-hand margin. Try to leave 2 or 3 cm of space between the last line and the bottom edge of the page.

Format of Manuscript

4

Put the title of your paper at the top of the first page of your manuscript — even though you may have put the title on a cover sheet. Do not use a period at the end of the title.

See **50** for instructions about how to set down the title of your paper.

5

Number all pages, after the first one, at the top of the page — either in the middle or at the right-hand margin.

Be sure to assemble the pages of your manuscript in the right sequence.

6

Secure your manuscript with a paper clip — *never* with a staple or pin.

Many editors will not accept a manuscript that is stapled together.

7

Use the proper kind of paper.

If you typewrite your manuscript, use white, unlined, opaque paper. If you handwrite your manuscript, use white, lined theme paper. Never submit a formal written assignment on pages torn from a spiral notebook.

Grammar

Introduction

Grammar may be defined as the study of how a language "works"—a study of how the structural system of a language combines with a vocabulary to convey meaning. When we study a foreign language in school, we must study both **vocabulary** and **grammar**, and until we can put the two together, we cannot translate the language. Sometimes we know the meaning of every word in a foreign-language sentence, and yet we cannot translate the sentence because we cannot figure out its grammar. On the other hand, we sometimes can figure out the syntax of the foreign-language sentence, but because we do not know the meaning of one or more words in the sentence, we still cannot translate the sentence.

If native speakers of English heard or read this sequence of words

> The porturbs in the brigger torms have tanted the makrets' rotment brokly.

they would perceive that the sequence bears a marked resemblance to an English sentence. Although many words in that sequence would be unfamiliar to them, they would detect that the sequence had the structure of the kind of

Grammar

English sentence that makes a statement, and they might further surmise that this kind of statement pattern was one that said that *porturbs* (whoever they are) had done something to *rotment* (whatever that is), or, to put it another way, that *porturbs* was the subject of the sentence, that *have tanted* was the predicate verb (transitive), and that *rotment* was the object of that transitive verb, the receiver of the action performed by the doer, *porturbs*. How were they able to make that much "sense" out of that sequence of strange words? They were able to detect that much "sense" by noting the following structural signals:

☐ Function words:
The three occurrences of the article **the;** the preposition **in;** and the auxiliary verb **have.**

☐ Inflections and affixes:
The **-s** added to nouns to form the plural; the **-er** added to adjectives to form the comparative degree; the **-ed** added to verbs to form the past tense or the past participle; the **-s'** added to nouns to form the plural possessive case; the affix **-ment** added to certain words to form an abstract noun; and the **-ly** added to adjectives to form adverbs.

☐ Word order:
The basic pattern of a statement or declarative sentence in English is S (subject) + V (verb) + C (complement) or NP (noun phrase) + VP (verb phrase). In the sequence, **The porturbs in the brigger torms** appears to be the S or NP part of the sentence and **have tanted the makrets' rotment brokly** the VP part of the sentence (**have tanted** being the V and **the makrets' rotment brokly** being the C).

☐ Intonation (stress, pitch, terminals, and juncture):
If the sequence were spoken aloud, native speakers would

detect that the sequence had the intonational pattern of a declarative sentence in spoken English.

☐ **Punctuation and mechanics:**
If the sequence were written out (as it is here), native speakers would observe that the sequence began with a capital letter and ended with a period, two typographical devices that signal a statement in written English.

Native speakers of English have been able to read all of this meaning into the string of nonsense words simply by observing the *grammatical* devices of **inflections, function words, word order,** and **intonation** (if spoken) or **punctuation** (if written). Now, if they had dictionaries that defined such words as *porturb, brig, torm, tant, makret, rotment,* and *brok*, they would be able to translate the full meaning of the sentence. But by observing the structural or grammatical devices alone, the native speakers of English will have perceived that the sequence of words

The porturbs in the brigger torms have tanted the makrets' rotment brokly.

exactly matches the structure of an English sentence like this one:

The citizens in the larger towns have accepted the politicians' commitment enthusiastically.

What they have been concentrating on is the *grammar* of the sentence, and it is in this sense that we use the term *grammar* in the section that follows.

Most children have mastered the fundamentals of this grammatical system of English by the time they start school. They have "mastered grammar" in the sense that they can form original and meaningful English sentences of their own

Grammar

and can understand English sentences uttered by others. They may not "know grammar" in the sense that they can analyze the structure of sentences and label the parts, but they know grammar in the sense that they can *perform appropriately* in the language—that is, that they can utter and respond to properly formed sentences.

In a sense, the grammar of a language is a convention. We formulate sentences in a certain way because communities of native speakers of the language, over a long period of time, have developed, and agreed on, certain ways of saying something. The grammar of a language allows some choices but forbids others. For instance, if you wanted to tell someone that a certain coach praised a certain player in a certain manner, grammar would allow you one of these choices of patterns:

> The coach praised the player enthusiastically.
> The coach enthusiastically praised the player.
> Enthusiastically the coach praised the player.
> The player was praised enthusiastically by the coach.

Grammar would not allow you to use one of these patterns:

> The player praised the coach enthusiastically.
> *(this is a grammatical sentence, but because of the altered word order, it does not say what you wanted it to say. Here the player is the doer of the action, and the coach is the receiver of the action)*
> The enthusiastically coach the player praised.
> Praised coach the enthusiastically player the

The choice of which grammatically acceptable pattern a writer will use is a concern of style, which will be dealt with in the next section.

8 Apostrophe for Possessive

In this section on grammar, we are dealing with those devices of *inflection, function words,* and *word order* that must be observed if written sentences are to convey the intended meaning to a reader clearly and unequivocally. We do not deal in this section with *intonation,* because this handbook is concerned only with the written language. In a later section of this handbook, we shall deal with the fourth grammatical device of written English, *punctuation.*

8

Use an apostrophe for the possessive, or genitive, case of the noun.

Here are some guidelines on forming the possessive, or genitive, case of the English noun:

(a) As indicated in the diagrams above, most English nouns form the possessive case with **'s** (singular) or **s'** (plural). (An alternative form of the possessive case consists of an **of** phrase: **the general's commands** or **the commands of the general.**)

(b) The possessive case of nouns that form their plurals in ways other than by adding an **s** is formed by adding **'s** to the plural of the noun: **man's/men's, woman's/women's, child's/children's, ox's/oxen's, deer's/deer's, mouse's/mice's.**

Grammar

(c) Some writers simply add an apostrophe to form the possessive case of nouns ending in **s**:

the actress' fame   Keats' odes
the alumnus' contribution   Dickens' death

However, other writers add the usual **'s** to form the possessive case of such nouns: **actress's, alumnus's** (plural, **alumni's**), **Keats's, Dickens's.** Take your choice, but be consistent.

(d) the rules for forming the possessive case of pairs of nouns are as follows: (1) in the case of joint possession, add **'s** only to the second member of the pair: **John and Mary's mother, the brother and sister's car;** and (2) in the case of individual possession, add **'s** to each member of the pair: **the boy's and girl's bedrooms, John's and Mary's tennis shoes, the men's and women's locker rooms.**

(e) Form the possessive case of group nouns and compound nouns by adding **'s** to the end of the unit: **commander in chief's, someone else's, president-elect's, editor in chief's, son-in-law's.** In the case of those compounds that form their plurals by adding **s** to the first word, form the plural possessive case by adding **'s** to the end of the unit: **editors in chief's, sons-in-law's.**

(f) Normally the **'s** or **'** is reserved for the possessive case of nouns naming animate creatures (human beings and animals). The **of** phrase is commonly used for the possessive case of inanimate nouns: not **the house's roof** but **the roof of the house.** Usage, however, now sanctions the use of **'s** with a number of inanimate nouns: **a day's wages, a week's work, the year's death toll, the school's policies, the car's performance, the radio's tone.**

10

9

**Its is the possessive case of the pronoun it;
it's is the contraction of it is or it has.**

Mistakes are frequently made with the pronoun **it**. The mistakes result from confusion about the two **s** forms of this pronoun. **It's** is used where **its** is the correct form **(X The dog broke it's leg** instead of ✔**The dog broke its leg), and its** is used where **it's** is the correct form **(X Its a shame that the girl broke her leg** instead of ✔**It's a shame that the girl broke her leg).**

Writers who use **it's** for the possessive case of **it** are probably influenced by the **'s** that is used to form the possessive case of the singular noun **(man's hat).** They might be able to avoid this mistake by remembering that none of the personal pronouns uses **'s** to form its possessive case: **I/my, you/your, he/his, she/her, it/its, we/our, they/their.** So they should write, **The company lost its lease.**

Or writers might be able to avoid this mistake if they remembered that the apostrophe has another function in written English: to indicate the omission of one or more letters in an English word, as in contractions **(I'll, don't, he'd).** The apostrophe in the word **it's** signals the contraction of the expression **it is** or **it has.** So they should write, **It's the first loss the company has suffered** or **It's come to my attention that you are frequently late.**

Don't let this little word defeat you. Get **it** right, once and for all.

Grammar

10

In any clause (dependent or independent), the predicate verb should agree in number with its subject.

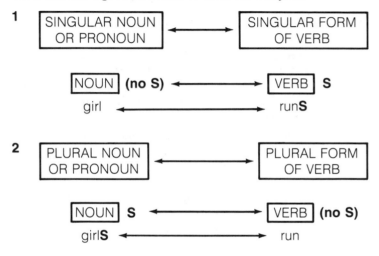

1

| SINGULAR NOUN OR PRONOUN | ←→ | SINGULAR FORM OF VERB |

NOUN (no S) ←→ VERB S
girl ←→ runS

2

| PLURAL NOUN OR PRONOUN | ←→ | PLURAL FORM OF VERB |

NOUN S ←→ VERB (no S)
girlS ←→ run

In addition to these differentiated forms of the verb in the third person, present tense, we have to be concerned about the few differentiated forms of the verb **to be (am/is/are; was/were)** and of auxiliary verbs **(has/have; does/do).**

The English verb has been evolving toward a single form for the singular and plural of all three persons (first, second, third)—as witness the **-ed** ending added to the verb in all three persons, singular and plural, of the past tense—and we may yet live to see the day when a totally simplified form of the English verb is achieved. In the meanwhile, the few remaining differentiated forms of the verb will probably continue to give writers some trouble.

10 Subject/Verb Agreement

Some typical examples of faulty agreement:

1 **X** He **don't** care about anything.
2 **X** The lawyer and his client **agrees** on a fee.
3 **X** If any one of the substations **are knocked** out, we can resort to reserve stations.
4 **X** The jury **has** made up **their** minds.
5 **X** He finds it impossible to live with the ignorance, injustice, poverty, and prejudice that **surrounds** him.
6 **X** Neither the gambler nor Jake **are** really bitter about their bad luck or **blame** anyone for their misfortunes.

Expressions like **He don't care about anything** are not so much "mistakes" in agreement as carry-overs from the dialect that people speak, quite acceptably, in their communities. People should be made aware, however, of the standard form of the verb in written prose: **He doesn't care about anything** (a singular verb with a singular subject).

Most errors of agreement in written prose are the result of carelessness, inadvertence, or uncertainty. Writers often know better; they merely slip up. Errors in agreement often occur when several words intervene between the simple subject of the sentence and the predicate verb, as in example **3** above: **If any one of the substations are knocked out** . . . . The simple subject of the **if** clause here is **one**, but because the plural noun **substations** (the object of the preposition **of**) intervened between that singular subject and the verb, the writer was influenced to use the plural form of the verb **(are knocked out)** instead of the correct singular form **(is knocked out).** Careful proofreading will often catch such inadvertent errors of agreement.

Errors due to uncertainty are another matter. Uncertainty about whether the verb should be singular or plural arises

Grammar

in cases where (1) the subject is compound; (2) the subject is a collective noun; (3) the subject of the sentence follows the structure **there is** or **there are;** and (4) the subject takes the form of structures like **one of those who** and **this man as well as.** Here are some guidelines for those puzzling cases:

(a) Compound subject

(1) Singular subjects joined by **and** usually take a plural verb.

John and his sister **were questioned** by the police.

(2) Singular subjects joined by **or** or by the correlative conjunctions **either ... or, neither ... nor** take a singular verb.

John or his sister **runs** the store during the week.

Neither the gambler nor Jake **is** really bitter about his bad luck or **blames** anyone for his misfortunes.

(3) When both subjects are plural, the verb is plural.

The detectives and the insurance agents **have expressed** their belief in the innocence of the brother and sister.

Neither the detectives nor the insurance agents **have expressed** any doubts about the innocence of the brother and sister.

(4) When one subject is singular and the other subject is plural and the subjects are joined by **or** or by the correlative conjunctions **either ... or, neither ... nor, both ... and, not only ... but also,** the verb agrees in number with the closest subject.

Either John or his parents **have agreed** to co-operate with the police.

Neither the brothers nor the sister **appears** to be co-operative.

10   Subject/Verb Agreement

However, plural or singular subjects joined by the correlative conjunctions **both ... and** or **not only ... but (also)** take a plural verb.

Both John and his sister **have agreed** to cooperate with the police.

Not only the brother but also the sister **appear** to be cooperative.

(b)   Collective noun as subject
(1)   If the collective noun is considered as a **group,** the verb is singular.

The jury **has made up** its mind.

The committee **was elected** unanimously.

The number of hockey players injured this winter **has increased** by 50 per cent.

(2)   If the collective noun is considered as **individuals** of a group, each acting separately, the verb is plural.

The jury **have made up** their minds.

The committee **wish** to offer their congratulations to the new chairperson.

A number of hockey players **have** petitioned the athletic board for better equipment.

(c)   The structure **there is/was, there was/ were**
(1)   If the delayed or real subject following the expletive **there** is singular, the verb is singular.

There **is** a remarkable consensus among the committee members.

(2)   If the delayed or real subject following the expletive **there** is plural, the verb is plural.

There **were** ten dissenting votes from the stockholders.

Grammar

(d) Special structures

(1) In the structure **one of the** (plural noun) **who,** the predicate verb of the **who** clause is plural, because the antecedent of the subject **who** is the plural noun rather than the singular **one.**

Matilda is one of the women who **refuse** to accept the ruling. *(here the antecedent of **who** is the plural noun **women**)*

(2) Exception: if **the only** precedes **one of the** (plural noun) **who,** the predicate verb of the **who** clause is singular, because the subject **who** in that case refers to the singular **one** rather than to the plural object of the preposition **of.**

Matilda is the only one of the women who **refuses** to accept the ruling.

(here the antecedent of **who** is the singular pronoun **one**)

(3) A singular subject followed by structures like **as well as, in addition to, together with** takes a singular verb.

(A plural subject, of course, followed by any of these structures, would take a plural verb. See the third example below.)

The sergeant as well as his superior officers **praises** his platoon.

Gill Dougal along with his roommate **has denied** the charges.

The students together with their counsellor **deny** that there has been any trouble during social activities.

(4) Nouns that do not end in *s* but that are plural in meaning take a plural verb.

The bacteria **require** constant attention.

These data **are** consistent with the judge's findings.

The deer **are running** loose in the state park.

16

10 Subject/Verb Agreement

(5) Nouns that end in *s* but that are singular in meaning take a singular verb.

Six passengers **is** too many for this boat to carry.

Ten dollars **is** a fair price for the coat.

Two weeks **seems** a long time when you are waiting for someone you love.

(6) Noun clauses serving as the subject of the sentence always take a singular verb.

That Sara decided to go to college **pleases** me very much.

What caused the accident **was** two stones in the road.

(7) In inverted structures, where the subject follows the verb, a singular subject takes a singular verb, and a plural subject takes a plural verb.

At each checkpoint **stands** a heavily armed soldier

Happy **were** they to see us arrive.

Among the crew **were** Carson, Barton, and Farmon.

Here are the corrected versions of all the sample sentences from page 13:

1 ✔ He **doesn't care** about anything.

2 ✔ The lawyer and her client **agree** on a fee.

3 ✔ If any one of the substations **is knocked** out, we can resort to reserve stations.

4 ✔ The jury **have made** up their minds.

5 ✔ He finds it impossible to live with the ignorance, injustice, poverty, and prejudice that **surround** him.

6 ✔ Neither the gambler nor Jake **is** really bitter about his bad luck or **blames** anyone for his misfortunes.

Grammar

11

A pronoun must agree in person, number, and gender with its antecedent noun.

Examples of faulty agreement between a pronoun and its antecedent:

1 X A **family** cannot go camping these days without a truckload of gadgets to make **your** campsite look just like home.

2 X The captain threw some floatable **items** overboard for the sailor, even though he knew that **it** would probably not save him.

3 X His **high school** did not live up to **his** promise to the students.

Pronouns, which are substitutes for nouns, have, in common with nouns **number** (singular and plural) and **gender** (masculine, feminine, and neuter). What nouns and pronouns do not share in common is the full range of **person.** All nouns are **third person** exclusively; but some pronouns are **first person (I, we),** some are **second person (you),** and some are **third person (e.g., he, she, it, they, one, some, none, all).**

A firm grammatical principle is that a pronoun must correspond with all the features of person, number, and gender it shares with its antecedent noun. A second-person pronoun cannot be linked with a third-person noun (see example **1** above); a singular pronoun cannot be linked with a plural noun (see example **2**); a masculine pronoun cannot be linked with a neuter noun (see example **3**).

Simple as the grammatical principle is that governs the relationship of a pronoun with its antecedent, there are a

11 Noun/Pronoun Agreement

few tricky problems for the writer in making a pronoun agree in person, number, and gender with its noun. For one thing, the English language has no convenient pronoun for indicating masculine-*or*-feminine gender. When a noun could be either masculine or feminine, writers sometimes have to use an awkward pronoun form like **his or her, his/her,** or **his (her),** as in the following sentence: Everyone should bring **his or her** schedule cards to the principal's office." Since these locutions are somewhat awkward, it is better to use a plural noun: "**Students** should bring **their** schedule cards to the principal's office."

Another problem stems from the ambiguity of **number** of such pronouns as **everyone, everybody, all, none, some, each.** Although there are exceptions, the following guidelines are generally reliable:

(a) **Everyone, everybody, anybody, anyone** invariably take singular verbs and, in formal usage at least, should be referred to by a singular pronoun.

Everyone in junior boys' basketball brings **his** schedule cards to the principal's office.
(formal usage)

(b) **All** and **some** are singular *or* plural according to the context. If the **of** phrase following the pronoun specifies a *mass* or *bulk* of something, the pronoun is singular; if the **of** phrase specifies a *number of things or persons,* the pronoun is plural.

Some of the fabric lost **its** coloring.

Some of the players turned in **their** amateur cards.

All of the players registered **their** complaints about the selection procedure.

Grammar

(c) None is singular or plural according to the context.
None of is generally singular; **none but** can often be singular or plural.

> None of the young men **was** willing to turn in **his** amateur card.
> None but teachers **are** allowed to park **their** cars in the lot.

(d) Each is almost invariably singular.

> Each of the women declared **her** allegiance to democracy.

Here are corrected versions of the sample sentences:

1 ✔ A family cannot go camping these days without a truckload of gadgets to make **their** [or **its**] campsite look just like home.
2 ✔ The captain threw some floatable **items** overboard for the sailor, even though he knew that **they** probably would not save him.
3 ✔ His **high school** did not live up to **its** promise to the students.

If you match up your pronouns in person, number, and gender with their antecedent nouns, you will make it easier for your reader to figure out what the pronouns refer to.

12

A pronoun should have a clear antecedent.

? . . . . PRONOUN

Examples of no antecedent or an unclear antecedent for the pronoun:

1 **X** Mayor Worthington, acting on the advice of her physician, resigned her office, and the city council, responding to a mandate from the voters, was swift to accept **it.**

(what did the council accept?)

12 Pronoun Antecedent

2 X John told his father that **his** car wouldn't start.

(whose car? the father's or John's?)

3 X I decided to break the engagement with my girlfriend, **which** distressed my parents very much.

(just what was it that distressed your parents?)

4 X The league's first major step was to sponsor a cleanup day, but **it** could not enlist enough volunteers.

*(a pronoun should not refer to a noun functioning as a possessive or as a modifier—here **league's**)*

5 X I enjoyed the sun and the sand and the surf, and **this** revealed to me that I really prefer a vacation at the beach.

*(what does **this** refer to?)*

Careless handling of the pronoun often blocks communication between writer and reader. The writer always knows what he or she meant the pronoun to stand for, but if there is no antecedent (a noun in the previous group of words to which the pronoun can refer) or if it is difficult to find the antecedent (the noun to which the pronoun refers), the reader will not know—and will have to guess—what the pronoun stands for.

A good piece of advice for apprentice writers is that whenever they use a pronoun, they should check to see whether there is a noun in the previous group of words that they could put in place of the pronoun. Let's apply this test to sentence **1.** There are three neuter, singular nouns to which the final pronoun **it** could refer: **advice, office, mandate.** But when we put each of these nouns, successively, in the place of **it,** we see that none of them names what the council accepted. If we pondered the sentence long enough, we might eventually figure out that what the council accepted was the mayor's *resignation.* But since the noun *resignation*

Grammar

appears nowhere in the sentence, the writer must use the noun phrase **her resignation** instead of the pronoun **it.** The revised version of sentence **1** will appear as follows: Mayor Worthington, acting on the advice of her physician, resigned her office, and the city council, responding to a mandate from the voters, was swift to accept **her resignation.**

Sentence **2** contains an example of an unclear anteced-ent. The pronoun reference is unclear because the pronoun **his** is ambiguous—that is, there are two nouns to which the masculine, singular pronoun **his** could refer: **John** and **father.** So we cannot tell whether it was the father's car or John's car that wouldn't start. If the context in which that sentence occurred did not help us determine whose car was being referred to, the writer could avoid the ambiguity by turning the sentence into a direct quotation: either **John told his father, "Your car won't start"** or **John told his father, "My car won't start."**

The use of the pronoun **this** or **that** to refer to a whole idea in a previous clause or sentence has long been a common practice in spoken English, and it is now becoming common in written English as well. Although the practice is gaining the approval of usage, writers should be aware that by using the demonstrative pronoun **this** or **that** to refer to a whole idea in the previous clause or sentence, they run the risk that the reference of the pronoun will be vague or ambiguous for their readers. If they do not want to run that risk, they can use **this** or **that** (or the corresponding plural, **these** or **those**) as an adjective instead of as a pronoun. The adjective would go before some noun summing up what **this** or **that** stands for. The writer of sentence **5** could avoid the vague pronoun reference by phrasing the sentence in this fashion: "I enjoyed the sun and the sand and the surf, and **this experience** revealed to me that I really prefer a vacation at the beach."

The use of the relative pronoun **which** or **that** to refer to a whole idea in the main clause rather than to a specific noun in that clause is also becoming more common. But there is a risk in this use similar to the one that attends the use of **this** or **that** to refer to a whole idea. The writer who worries about whether the reader will be even momentarily baffled by the **which** in a sentence like **3** will supply a summary noun to serve as the antecedent for that relative pronoun: "I decided to break the engagement with my girlfriend, a **decision which** distressed my parents very much."

The problem with the pronoun reference in sentence **4** stems from the linguistic fact that a pronoun does not readily reveal its antecedent if it refers to a noun that is functioning in a subordinate structure such as a possessive (the **school's** principal), a modifier of a noun (the **school** term), or an object of a preposition (in the **school**). One remedy for the vague pronoun reference in sentence **4** is to use the noun **league** rather than the pronoun **it** ". . . but the **league** could not enlist enough volunteers." A better remedy is to make **league** the subject of the first clause so that the **it** in the second clause would have an antecedent: "The **league** took its first major step by sponsoring a cleanup day, but **it** could not enlist enough volunteers."

The writer who has mastered the use of the pronoun has mastered a good part of the craft of writing lucid prose.

Grammar

13

An introductory verbal or verbal phrase must find its "doer" in the subject of the main clause.

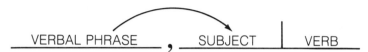

| VERBAL PHRASE | **,** | SUBJECT | VERB |

Examples of "dangling" verbal phrases:

1 X Walking on the sidewalk, the Volkswagen ran over me.
2 X By returning evil for evil, no permanent good can be accomplished.
3 X Refusing to be inducted into the army, the World Boxing Association stripped Muhammed Ali of his title.
4 X To accomplish this end, it is necessary for us to study grammar and usage.

In English, an introductory verbal or verbal phrase (participles, gerunds, and infinitives) naturally adheres to the subject of the main clause. When the subject of the main clause is not the "doer" of the action indicated in the verbal, we say that the verbal **dangles**—that it is not attached to the proper agent. By ignoring this basic principle of English grammar, writers often produce ludicrous sentences, like the first example above, and say what they did not intend to say.

To prevent dangling verbals, the writer should make sure that the subject of the main clause is the *doer* of the action specified in the preceding verbal. If the writers of the sample sentences above had observed this caution, they would have revised their sentences to read:

14   Misplaced Modifier

1 ✔ Walking on the sidewalk, I was run over by a Volkswagen. **OR:** A Volkswagen ran over me while I was walking on the sidewalk.
2 ✔ By returning evil for evil, one can accomplish no permanent good.
3 ✔ Refusing to be inducted into the army, Muhammed Ali was stripped of his title by the World Boxing Association. **OR:** The World Boxing Association stripped Muhammed Ali of his title for refusing to be inducted into the army.
4 ✔ To accomplish this end, we must study grammar and usage.

14

Misplaced modifiers lead to a misreading of the sentence.

Examples of misplaced modifiers:

1 X Anyone who reads a newspaper **frequently** will notice that many people are now concerned about pollution.
2 X The author seems to be saying that people who refer to the past **constantly** follow the same ritual themselves.
3 X He has **only** a face that a mother could love.
4 X The teacher distributed examinations to the students **covered with splotches of ink.**
5 X **After you entered the park,** the sponsors of the Summerfest decided that you would not have to spend any more money at the concession stands.
6 X The plot of the story is a simple one, but there is little chance of the reader becoming bored **because the author uses many clever devices to advance the plot.**

Grammar

Because English is a language that depends heavily on word order, related words must often be placed as close as possible to one another. Adverbial and adjectival modifiers especially must be placed as close as possible to words that they modify. Failure to juxtapose related words often leads to a misreading, to a reading different from what the writer intended.

In sample sentences **1** and **2** above, we have examples of what are called **squinting modifiers,** modifiers that look in two directions at once. In sentence **1**, the adverb **frequently** is sitting between two verbs that grammatically and semantically it could modify—**reads** and **will notice.** If the writers intend the adverb to modify the act of reading rather than the act of noticing, they should shift the position of **frequently** so that the sentence reads as follows: **Anyone who frequently reads a newspaper will notice that many people are now concerned about pollution.** If, however, they intend the adverb to modify the act of noticing, they should shift **frequently** to a position between **will** and **notice** or after **notice.**

In sample sentence **2**, the adverb **constantly** is likewise sitting between two verbs that it could modify—**refer** and **follow**. Shifting the adverb to a position before the verb **refer** will make the sentence say what the writer probably meant it to say: **The author seems to be saying that people who constantly refer to the past follow the same ritual themselves.**

Because **only** in the third sample sentence is placed in the wrong clause in the sentence, it modifies **a face.** The writer of that sentence could avoid eliciting chuckles from readers by putting **only** in the clause where it belongs and making the sentence read as follows: **He has a face that only a mother could love.**

Notice how shifting the position of the modifiers in sample sentences **3**, **4**, **5**, and **6** makes the sentences say what they were intended to say:

3 ✔ He has a face that only a mother could love.

4 ✔ The teacher distributed to the students examinations covered with splotches of ink.

5 ✔ The sponsors of the Summerfest decided that after you entered the park you would not have to spend any more money at the concession stands.

6 ✔ The plot of the story is a simple one, but because the author uses many clever devices to advance the plot, there is little chance of the reader becoming bored.

Reading sentences aloud will sometimes reveal the misplacement of modifying words, phrases, and clauses.

15

Preserve parallel structure by using units of the same grammatical kind.

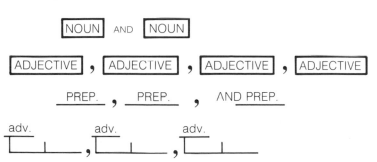

Grammar

Examples of breakdown in parallelism:

1 X The old beliefs about theft have been rejected as **superstitions** and **detrimental** to one's prestige.
(noun and adjective)

2 X He was a **miser,** a **bachelor,** and **egotistical.**
(noun, noun, adjective)

3 X John was **healthy, wealthy,** and an **athlete.**
(adjective, adjective, noun)

4 X First of all, Daisy was an **adult, married,** and **had a young daughter.**
(noun, adjective, verb phrase)

5 X Lincoln was a man **of the people, for the people,** and **loved by the people.**
(prepositional phrase, prepositional phrase, participial phrase)

6 X The foreman commended the steelworkers **for their patriotism** and **because they did not ask for a wage increase.**
(prepositional phrase, adverb clause)

7 X I enjoy reading simply **for personal enlightenment** and **to develop mental sharpness.**
(prepositional phrase, infinitive phrase)

8 X The advertisers **not only** convince the reader that the Cadillac is a luxury car **but also** that the car confers status on its owner.
(violation of parallelism with correlative conjunctions)

The principle governing parallel structure is that a pair or a series (three or more) of co-ordinate units should be of the same kind—nouns with nouns, adjectives with adjectives, not a mixture of nouns and adjectives. A breakdown in parallelism wrenches coherence because it disrupts the expectation that is set up for a reader when a series starts out with one kind of unit and then suddenly shifts to another kind.

15 Parallelism

The obvious way to correct a breakdown in parallelism is to convert all the members of the pair or the series to units of the same grammatical kind. Let us first correct all the violations of parallelism in the sample sentences and then comment on the revisions.

1 ✔ The old beliefs about theft have been rejected as **superstitious** and **detrimental** to one's prestige.

(adjective and adjective)

2 ✔ He was a **miser,** a **bachelor,** and an **egotist.**

(noun, noun, noun)

3 ✔ John was **healthy, wealthy,** and **athletic.**

(adjective, adjective, adjective)

4 ✔ First of all, Daisy was an **adult,** a married **woman,** and the **mother** of a young daughter.

(noun, noun, noun)

5 ✔ Lincoln was a man **who was born of the people, who worked for the people,** and **who was loved by the people.**

(adjective clause, adjective clause, adjective clause)

6 ✔ The foreman commended the steelworkers **for their patriotism** and **for their restraint.**

(prepositional phrase, prepositional phrase)

7 ✔ I enjoy reading simply **to gain personal enlightenment** and **to develop mental sharpness.**

(infinitive phrase, infinitive phrase)

8 ✔ The advertisers convince the reader not only **that the Cadillac is a luxury car** but also **that the car confers status on its owner.**

(noun clause, noun clause)

In converting all the members of a pair or a series to units of the same grammatical kind, a writer sometimes has an

Grammar

either/or choice available, but usually one of the options will be stylistically preferable to the other. In sentences **2, 6,** and **7,** the writer could have chosen another option:

2 ✔ He was **miserly, single,** and **egotistical.**

6 ✔ The foreman commended the steelworkers **because they were patriotic and because they did not ask for a wage increase.**

7 ✔ I enjoy reading simply **for personal enlightenment** and **for mental sharpness.**

Whenever alternative ways of repairing the breakdown in parallelism are available, the writer has to exercise judgement in deciding which is the better stylistic choice in a particular case.

Sentences **1, 3,** and **4,** however, do not readily lend themselves to alternative revisions. In sentence **1,** for instance, the writer could convert the pair to two nouns (**superstitions** and **detriments**), but that wording is not as stylistically satisfactory as the conversion to two adjectives (**superstitious** and **detrimental**). The predicate terms in sentence **3** cannot be converted to three nouns because there are no single-word noun equivalents of the adjectives **healthy** and **wealthy** that can be used to describe John; so this sentence can be made parallel only by turning all three units into adjectives. The use of noun phrases was the only option available for the revision of sentence **4** because there is no noun or adjective equivalent of the verb phrase **had a young daughter.**

Correcting the violation of parallelism in sentence **5** was almost impossible because of the unavailability of three equivalent prepositional phrases or three equivalent participial phrases. The best that could be done in that case was to use three **who** clauses, but even though that revision makes the sentence grammatically parallel, it is not stylistically satisfactory.

Sentence **8** illustrates a violation of parallelism when correlative conjunctions are used: **either . . . or; neither . . . nor; not (only) . . but (also).** The principle operating with correlative conjunctions is that the same grammatical structure must be on the right-hand side of both conjunctions. We can more easily see the breakdown in parallelism if we lay out sentence **8** in two layers:

The advertisers **not only** convince the reader that the Cadillac is a luxury car
but also that the car confers status on its owner.

On the right-hand side of **not only**, the writer has this grammatical sequence: a verb (**convince**), a noun (**the reader**), and a noun clause (**that the Cadillac is a luxury car**). On the right-hand side of **but also**, however, the writer has *only* the noun clause (**that the car confers status on its owner**). The faulty parallelism can be revised in either of two ways:

The advertisers **not only** convince the reader that the Cadillac is a luxury car
but also convince the reader that the car confers status on its owner.

The advertisers convince the reader **not only** that the Cadillac is a luxury car
but also that the car confers status on its owner.

In both revisions, we now have the same grammatical structures on the right-hand side of both correlative conjunctions. But because the second revision has fewer words and less repetition than the first one, it is probably the better of the two revisions.

Grammar

Note how parallelism is preserved in the following two sentences using correlative conjunctions:

- 🖊 **Either** he will love the one and hate the other, **or** he will hate the one and love the other.
- 🖊 He will **either** love the one and hate the other **or** hate the one and love the other.

The principle governing parallelism: **like must be joined with like.**

16

Use the subordinating conjunction <u>that</u> if it will prevent a possible misreading.

Examples where it would be advisable to insert **that:**

1 My father believed‸his doctor, who was a boyhood friend, was wholly trustworthy.
2 A more realistic person would probably assert‸these statements about the ad were frivolous and sentimental.
3 He discovered‸the radio and the tape recorder in his roommate's closet had been stolen.
4 Professor Clements maintained‸communism rejected capitalism and democracy rejected collective ownership.

The tendency of any language is toward economy of means. So we omit syllables in such contractions as **he's, she'll, we'd, won't,** and we resort to such common elliptical expressions as **he is taller than I (am tall); when (I was) in the fourth grade, I went to the zoo with my father.** We also frequently omit the conjunction **that,** which introduces a noun clause serving as the object of a verb, as in "He said he was going" and "He announced I was a candidate for office."

Whether to use the conjunction **that** in written prose will be a problem only when a noun clause is being used as the direct object of a verb—but not in every instance of such use. If there is no chance that the syntax of a sentence will be misread, it is all right, even in written prose, to omit **that.** But if there is a chance that a noun phrase following the verb may be read as the object of the verb rather than as the subject of the subsequent clause, then the writer should prevent even a momentary misreading by inserting **that** at the beginning of the noun clause. What follows may make all of this clearer.

In a sentence like **He said he was going,** it is safe to omit **that** after **said** because **he,** being a pronoun in the nominative case (see GLOSSARY), cannot possibly be read as the object of **said.** But in a sentence like sample sentence **1** in this section, it is not only possible, but also likely that the noun phrase **his doctor** will momentarily be read as the object of **believed (he believed his doctor).** Of course, as soon as readers come to the predicate **was wholly trustworthy,** they realize that they have misread the sentence, and they have to back up and reread the sentence as the writer intended it to be read. But the writer could have prevented that initial misreading by inserting **that** after **believed—My father believed that his doctor, who was a boyhood friend, was wholly trustworthy.** Then the sentence can be read in only one way—the way in which the writer intended it to be read.

Note how the insertion of **that** where the caret (∧) is in the other sample sentences prevents an initial misreading of the sentences. Whenever a reader has to reread a sentence in

Grammar

order to make sense of it, the writer is usually the one to blame. Inserting **that** where it is necessary or advisable will save the reader from having to reread a sentence.

17

Avoid the careless or indefensible use of sentence fragments.

Examples of questionable sentence fragments:

1 X **The reason for this reaction being that people are flattered by courtesy.**

2 X I shall not try to defend myself on the grounds that I did not violate the regulation. **Although I could offer the excuse that I didn't know that such a regulation existed.**

3 X Both men are alike in that they try to help people only if the effort does not result in too much trouble for themselves. **Herenger, in his idea that it is good to help someone with "so little trouble to himself," and the Baron, who believes in giving money to someone as long as there is no further responsibility involved.**

4 X Much information about a topic can be brought forth by poetry. **The topic of science, in particular, because science is basically factual.**

A sentence fragment can be defined as a string of words, between an initial capital letter and a period or question mark, that lacks a subject or a finite-verb predicate (or both) or that has a subject and a finite-verb predicate but is made part of a larger structure by a relative pronoun **(who, which, that)** or by a subordinating conjunction **(because, if, when,** etc.).

The string of words in example **1** above is a sentence fragment because the subject **reason** lacks a finite-verb predicate. Changing the participle **being** to the finite verb **is** would make that string of words a complete sentence.

The boldface string of words in example **2** is a sentence fragment because the subordinating conjunction **although** makes the clause that follows it a part of, or dependent on, a larger structure. The adverb clause introduced by **although** "depends on" the independent clause in the previous sentence, and therefore the adverb clause cannot stand by itself. This example may be more the result of carelessness in punctuating the sentence than the result of ignorance of what constitutes a complete sentence, for the sentence fragment here can be eliminated simply by changing the period after **regulation** to a comma and reducing the first letter in **Although** to lower case **(I shall not try to defend myself on the grounds that I did not violate the regulation, although I could offer the excuse that I didn't know that such a regulation existed).**

The boldface string of words in example **3** is a sentence fragment because it lacks an independent clause. It lacks an independent clause because neither **Herenger** nor **Baron,** which appear to be "subjects," has a predicate verb. With predicate verbs this fragment would become a sentence: **Herenger's willingness to help someone "with so little trouble to himself" is similar to the Baron's belief in giving money to someone as long as there is no further responsibility involved.** Likewise **The topic of science** in **4** lacks a predicate verb. With a predicate verb, number **4** would read: **The topic of science, in particular, lends itself to poetic treatment, because science is basically factual.**

Grammar

Whether a string of words constitutes a complete sentence or only a sentence fragment is a grammatical concern; whether the use of a sentence fragment is appropriate in a particular context and is therefore justifiable is a rhetorical or stylistic concern. It is a fact of life that sometimes we communicate with one another in sentence fragments. Take for instance the following exchange:

Where are you going tonight?	What time?
The movies.	About eight-thirty.
With whom?	By car?
Jack.	No, by bus.
Where?	Can I go along?
The Palace.	Sure.

Once the context of that dialogue was established, both speakers communicated with one another in fragments. Notice, though, that the dialogue had to be initiated by a complete sentence (the question **Where are you going tonight?**) and that later the first speaker had to resort again to a complete sentence **(Can I go along?)** because there was no way to phrase that question clearly in a fragmentary way.

Native speakers of a language can converse in fragments because each of them is capable of mentally supplying what is missing from an utterance. When in response to the initial question the second speaker answers, "The movies," that phrase conveys a meaning because the first speaker is able to supply, mentally and perhaps subconsciously, the missing elements in the fragmentary reply: **(I am going to) the movies.**

All of us have encountered sentence fragments in the written prose of some very reputable writers. Predicateless sentences are most likely to be found in mood-setting descriptive and narrative prose, as in this paragraph of John Steinbeck's novel *The Grapes of Wrath:*

> Along 66 the hamburger stands—Al & Susy's Place—Carl's Lunch—Joe & Minnie—Will's Eats. Board-and-bat shacks. Two gasoline pumps in front, a screen door, a long bar, stools, and a foot rail. Near the door three slot machines, showing through glass the wealth in nickels three bars will bring. And beside them, the nickel phonograph with records piled up like pies, ready to swing out to the turntable and play dance music, "Ti-pi-ti-pi-tin," "Thanks for the Memories," Bing Crosby, Benny Goodman. At one end of the counter a covered case; candy cough drops, caffeine sulphate called Sleepless, No-Doze; candy, cigarettes, razor blades, aspirin, Bromo-Seltzer, Alka-Seltzer. The walls decorated with posters, bathing girls, blondes with big breasts and slender hips and waxen faces, in white bathing suits, and holding a bottle of Coca-Cola and smiling—see what you get with a Coca-Cola. Long bar, and salts, peppers, mustard pots, and paper napkins. Beer taps behind the counter, and in back the coffee urns, shiny and steaming, with glass gauges showing the coffee level. And pies in wire cages and oranges in pyramids of four. And little piles of Post Toasties, corn flakes, stacked up in designs.

In that paragraph, there are no clauses (that is, groups of words with a subject and a finite-verb predicate); the paragraph is composed predominantly of nouns and noun phrases. But although the passage is lacking in predications made by finite verbs, the sequence of sentence fragments creates effects that Steinbeck could not have achieved—or could not achieved as well—with complete sentences.

The point of citing these examples of spoken and written discourse is that sentence fragments are a part of the English language (in that sense they are "grammatical"), that in certain contexts they do communicate meaning, and that in some circumstances and for some purposes they are

Grammar

appropriate and therefore acceptable, effective, and even stylistically desirable. But writers should be aware of what they are doing. They should know that they are writing sentence fragments rather than complete sentences, otherwise they will be guilty of *careless* use of sentence fragments. And they should have some purpose or effect in mind when they use a sentence fragment; otherwise they will be guilty of *indefensible* use of sentence fragments.

18

Independent clauses cannot be spliced together simply with a comma.

Examples of comma splices:

1 X We are not allowed to think for ourselves **,** that privilege is reserved for administrators.

2 X Last summer my family saw the whole of Canada from the inside of an air-conditioned trailer **,** outside the weather ranged from cool to hot, from dry to muggy.

3 X Our minds are never challenged by the television set **,** it is just so much easier to sit there than to read a book.

4 X You will have to choose your vocation yourself **,** however, you should consider what others have told you about the hazards of various jobs.

18 Comma Splice

A comma splice is the joining of independent clauses with a comma. It occurs only in compound sentences—that is, in sentences composed of two or more independent clauses. A comma splice is an error in punctuation; but since punctuation is, for the written language, the equivalent of vocal intonation in the spoken language, this error in punctuation can also be considered an error in grammar.

Independent clauses must be joined either by a co-ordinating conjunction **(and, but, or, for, nor, yet, so)** or by a semicolon. In addition to these two ways of properly splicing independent clauses, there are two other ways of fixing up the comma splice: by making separate sentences of the two clauses and by subordinating one of the clauses. Using each of these methods in turn, let us correct the comma splice in sample sentence **1** above.

(a) Insert the appropriate co-ordinating conjunction after the comma:

We are not allowed to think for ourselves, **for** that privilege is reserved for administrators.

(b) Substitute a semicolon for the comma:

We are not allowed to think for ourselves **;** that privilege is reserved for administrators.

(c) Subordinate one of the independent clauses:

We are not allowed to think for ourselves, **because** that privilege is reserved for administrators.

(d) Put a period at the end of the first independent clause and begin a new sentence with the first word of the second independent clause:

We are not allowed to think for ourselves • **T**hat privilege is reserved for administrators.

Grammar

Although these four ways of fixing up a comma splice are always available, one of these options will usually be best in a particular instance. In the case of sample sentence **1**, splicing the two clauses together with a semicolon would probably be best: **We are not allowed to think for ourselves; that privilege is reserved for administrators.** The semicolon here effects the closest union of the two related clauses and best points up the irony between the thoughts in the two clauses. We have made our choice of the semicolon on stylistic grounds; grammatically, the other three options are equally correct. Sentences **2, 3,** and **4** may also be corrected either by splicing their clauses together with a semicolon or by turning the commas into periods and creating two sentences.

See **40** and **41** in the punctuation section for the proper use of the semicolon.

19

Do not run independent clauses together without a conjunction or the proper punctuation.

Examples of independent clauses run together:

1 **X** Why am I qualified to speak on this subject I just finished three dreadful years of high school.
2 **X** Those shiny red apples sitting on my desk pleased me very much they were tokens of affection from my students.

3 X Two suspects were arrested last week one of them was a cripple.

4 X Leggatt was convicted for having killed a man thus he would never be able to work on a ship again.

The term commonly used to label two or more independent clauses that have been run together without any conjunction or punctuation is **fused sentence** or **run-on sentence.** Fused sentences are not as common in writing as comma splices, but when they do occur, they are even more of a stumbling block for a reader than comma splices are. If the writers of the sample sentences above had read their string of words aloud, they would have detected a natural stopping place— a place where the expression of one thought ended and the expression of another thought began.

Fused sentences can be corrected in the same four ways that comma splices can be corrected:

(a) Join the independent clauses with the appropriate co-ordinating conjunction:

✔ Those shiny red apples sitting on my desk pleased me very much, **for** they were tokens of affection from my students.

(b) Splice the independent clauses with a semicolon:

✔ Two suspects were arrested last week **;** one of them was a cripple.

(c) Subordinate one of the independent clauses:

✔ **Because** Leggatt was convicted for having killed a man, he would never be able to work on a ship again.

(d) Make separate sentences of the independent clauses:

✔ Why am I qualified to speak on this subject **?** I just finished three dreadful years of high school.

Grammar

As in the case of comma splices, all four of these ways are usually available for correcting a fused sentence, but in a particular instance, one of them will usually be better than the others. Some of the sample sentences do not readily lend themselves to correction by all four means. For instance because sample sentence **1** fuses a question and a statement—**Why am I qualified to speak on this subject** (question) and **I just finished three dreadful years of high school** (statement)—it lends itself to correction only by the fourth method, that of making separate sentences of the two clauses.

Reading one's prose aloud will usually disclose instances where independent clauses have been run together.

20

Choose words and put them together so that they make sense.

Examples of confused or puzzling sentences:

1 X Much later in the story, the dinner conversation the function of the "small talk" seems to be about the old times.

2 X The youth, rejected by his parents, by the world, by God, and tragically and ultimately he has rejected himself.

3 X Margaret Laurence presents in her novel *The Fire Dwellers* as extraordinary an ordinary person as an ordinary person could be in an ordinary environment.

4 X Now in the third stanza, the poet starts his descent. He brings about his conclusion of the boy, which can be paralleled to humanity.

5 X Of course, this situation of rundown houses is not always the case, but instead the high rent that the tenants have to pay, which leaves little money for anything else.

20 Confusing Sentence

A confused or puzzling sentence is one that because of some flaw in the choice or disposition of words reveals no meaning or only a vague meaning. We could say of such a sentence that it is a "non-English" sentence—a sentence that is semantically or grammatically impossible in the English language. A sentence like "That bachelor is a happily married man" is a strange sentence because **bachelor** and **married man** are incompatible. The phrase **his conclusion of the boy** in sample sentence **4** is another instance of a choice of incompatible words. A sentence like "Harshly me teacher scolded the yesterday" is a non-English sentence because English grammar does not allow that order of words. To make sense, those words have to be disposed in an order like this: **The teacher scolded me harshly yesterday.** Each of the first, second, third, and fifth sample sentences has some flaw in syntax that prevents the writer's meaning from getting through to the reader.

If readers cannot figure out what the writer meant to say, they often cannot analyze what went wrong with the sentence, and they certainly cannot suggest how the bewildering sentence might be fixed up. The best they can do is to point out that the sentence makes no sense and urge the writer to rephrase it.

In the following revisions, (1) a guess has been made about what the author meant to say, (2) as many of the original words as possible have been retained, and (3) none of the needed stylistic changes has been made. We have merely tried to repair the sentences so that they make some kind of sense.

1 ✓ Much later in the story—during the dinner conversation—the function of the "small talk" seems to be to recall the old times.

Grammar

2 ✔ The youth, rejected by his parents, by the world, by God, has tragically and ultimately rejected himself.

3 ✔ Margaret Laurence presents in her novel *The Fire Dwellers* an extraordinary person in an ordinary environment.

4 ✔ Now in the third stanza, the poet starts his descent. He draws his conclusion about the boy, which s similar to the generalization that could be made about the rest of humanity.

5 ✔ Of course, the houses are not invariably rundown, but the high rent that the tenants have to pay leaves little money for anything else.

If reading sentences aloud to oneself does not help in detecting confused or puzzling sentences, it may be necessary to read them aloud to someone else.

Style

Introduction

Style is the result of the choices that a writer makes from the available vocabulary and syntactical resources of a language. A writer may not choose—or should not choose

☐ Words and structures that are not part of the language.

The defendants have **klinded** the case to the Supreme Court.

(no such word in the English language)

All gas stations **having being closed** for the duration of the emergency.

(no such verb structure in the English language)

☐ Words and structures that make no sense:

The mountains lucidly transgressed sentient rocks.

(a grammatical but nonsensical sentence)

☐ Words and structures that convey ambiguous meanings:

The teacher gave the papers to the students that were chosen by the committee.

*(was it the **papers** or the **students** that were chosen by the committee?)*

Aside from these unavailable or inadvisable choices, however, the rich vocabulary and the flexible syntax of the English language offer the writer a number of alternative but

Style

synonymous ways of saying something. One may choose to use an active verb or a passive verb:

He reported the accident to the police.

OR: The accident was reported by him to the police.

or one may shift the position of some modifiers:

He reported the accident to the police when he was ready.

OR: When he was ready, he reported the accident to the police.

or one may substitute synonymous words and phrases:

He informed the police about the accident at the intersection.

OR: John notified Constable James Murphy about the collision at the corner of Fifth and Main.

A number of other stylistic choices may be open to the writer:

(a) whether to write a long sentence or to break up the sentence into a series of short sentences.
(long sentence)

In a sense, we did not have history until the invention of the alphabet, because before that invention, the records of national events could be preserved only if there were bards inspired enough to sing about those events and audiences patient enough to listen to a long, metered recitation.

OR

(a series of short sentences)

In a sense, we did not have history until the invention of the alphabet. Before that invention, the records of national events were passed on by singing bards. But those bards had to have audiences patient enough to listen to a long, metered recitation.

(b) whether to write a compound sentence or to subordinate one of the clauses.

(compound sentence)

None of the elegies that were delivered at funerals in eighteenth-century village churches has been preserved, but the "short and simple annals of the poor" have been preserved on thousands of gravestones from that era.

OR

(subordinate one of the clauses)

Although none of the elegies that were delivered at funerals in eighteenth-century village churches has been preserved, the "short and simple annals of the poor" have been preserved on thousands of gravestones from that era.

(c) whether to modify a noun with an adjective clause or with a participial phrase or merely with an adjective.

(adjective clause)

The house, which was painted a garish red, did not find a buyer for two months.

OR

(participial phrase)

The house, painted a garish red, did not find a buyer for two months.

OR

(adjective)

The garishly red house did not find a buyer for two months.

(d) whether to use literal language or figurative language.

Style

(literal)
The prime minister walked into a room filled with angry reporters.

OR

(figurative)

The prime minister walked into a hornet's nest.

(e) whether to use a "big" word or an ordinary word *(altercation* or *quarrel)*, a specific word or a general word *(sauntered* or *walked)*, a formal word or a colloquial word *(children* or *kids)*.

(big, formal words)

Everyone was astonished by her phenomenal equanimity.

OR

(ordinary, colloquial words)

Everyone was flabbergasted by her unusual cool.

(f) whether to begin a succession of sentences with the same word and the same structure or to vary the diction and the structure.

(same word, same structure)

We wanted to preserve our heritage. We wanted to remind our children of our national heroes. We wanted to inspire subsequent generations to emulate our example.

OR

(different words, different structures)

We wanted to preserve our heritage. Our children, in turn, needed to be reminded of our national heroes. Could we inspire subsequent generations to emulate our example?

Introduction

The availability of options such as these gives writers the opportunity to achieve variety in their style. *By varying the length, the rhythm, and the structure of their sentences, writers can avoid monotony, an attention-deadening quality in prose.*

Choice is the key word in connection with style. Some choices a writer may not, or should not, make. As was pointed out at the beginning of this section, a writer may not choose what the grammar of the language does not allow. Furthermore, a writer cannot choose resources of language he or she does not command. A writer would also be ill-advised to choose words and structures that are inappropriate for the subject matter, the occasion, or the audience.

Aside from those constraints, however, a writer has hundreds of decisions to make about the choice of vocabulary or syntax while writing. Grammar will determine whether a particular stylistic choice is *correct*—that is, whether a particular locution complies with the conventions of the language. Rhetoric will determine whether a particular stylistic choice is *effective*—that is, whether a particular locution conveys the intended meaning with the clarity, economy, emphasis, and tone appropriate to the subject matter, occasion, audience, and desired effect.

The previous section dealt with what the grammar of the language permits—or, more accurately, with what the conventions of Canadian English Usage permit. This section on style will guide writers in making judicious choices from among the available options. Questions about style are not so much questions about *right* and *wrong* as questions about *good, better, best.*

Style

21

Choose the right word or expression for what you intend to say.

Examples of wrong words:

1 X The typical lifeguard has long **ignominious** hair bleached by the **torpid** sun.

2 X By the time we reached Toronto, we had spent our food allotment and were faced with the gloomy **aspect** of starving to death.

3 X If you do not **here** from me within three weeks, give me a call.

4 X The equator is a **menagerie lion** running around the earth.

A word is labelled "wrong" when its meaning does not fit the context, does not express the intended meaning. The most obvious instance of a "wrong word" is the substitution, usually due to carelessness, of a homonym (a like-sounding word) for the intended word, like **here** for **hear** (see example **3** above), **through** for **threw, there** for **their, sole** for **soul.**

Another kind of "wrong word" is what is called a **malapropism,** after Mrs. Malaprop in Sheridan's play *The Rivals.* Mrs. Malaprop would say things like "as headstrong as an *allegory* on the banks of the Nile." There is a malapropism in example **4.** The writer has heard the expression "imaginary line," but by using the approximate-sounding words **menagerie lion,** he or she has produced a "howler." **Aspect** in example **2** makes some sense, but *prospect* would come closer to expressing what the writer probably had in mind.

The most common kind of "wrong word" is usually the result of a writer's using a word that is new and somewhat unfamiliar. In example **1,** the denotative meaning of **ignominious** is "disgraceful, shameful," but although we can speak of "an ignominious act," the word is inappropriate

21 Wrong Word and Faulty Predication

when attached to **hair.** In the same sentence, if the writer meant to say that the sun was sluggish, **torpid** is the right word; but "torrid sun" comes closer to what was probably meant.

Another common instance of "wrong word" can be designated by the term **faulty predication.** A faulty predication occurs when the predicate of a clause (either the verb itself or the whole verb phrase) does not fit semantically or syntactically with the subject of a clause. In other words, the predicate of a clause must fit *grammatically* with the subject (e.g., see sample sentences **8**, **9**, and **10** below) and must be compatible *in meaning* with the subject (e.g., see sample sentence **1** below). Here are some examples of incompatible predicates:

1 **X** A thief and a liar **are vices** that we should avoid.

2 **X** His purpose **was a ridicule and exposure** of the business mentality.

3 **X** The first section of the poem **is** nothing more than Dryden's reasons for liking Mr. Oldham.

4 **X** He cited an article that **was a dual authorship.**

5 **X** Edgar Lee Masters is saying that the shootings and the hangings are indefensible and that justice **seems** only for the rich.

6 **X** Abused children **should not be tolerated** in our society.

7 **X** The source of Morley Callaghan's title *They Shall Inherit the Earth* is taken from a verse in the New Testament.

8 **X** The reason she did not come to class **is because she was sick.**

9 **X** The beach **is where I get my worst sunburn.**

10 **X** An example of honesty **is when someone finds a wallet and takes it to the police.**

Faulty predications often occur when some form of the verb **to be** serves as the predicate verb, as in the first four examples and in the last three. Because the verb **to be** is

Style

setting up an equation between the subject and the complement, the complement part of the sentence must fit semantically and syntactically with the subject part of the sentence. In example **1**, for instance, the complement **vices** does not fit semantically with the subject **a thief and a liar** (thieves and liars are not vices). The adverb clauses following the verb **to be** in examples **8**, **9**, and **10** do not fit syntactically, because adverb clauses cannot serve as complements for the verb **to be** (no more than a simple adverb could serve as the complement for the verb **to be:** "he is swiftly".) The examples **5**, **6**, and **7** above are instances of faulty predication with verbs other than the verb **to be.**

Revisions of the faulty predications:

1. ✔ A thief and a liar exemplify (or practise) vices that we should avoid. (Or: Thievery and lying are vices that we should avoid.)

2. ✔ His purpose was to ridicule and expose the business mentality.

3. ✔ The first section of the poem presents nothing more than Dryden's reasons for liking Mr. Oldham.

4. ✔ He cited an article that had a dual authorship. (Or: He cited an article that was written by two authors.)

5. ✔ Edgar Lee Masters is saying that the shootings and the hangings are indefensible and that justice seems to be reserved only for the rich.

6. ✔ Abused children should be removed from their parents. (Or: The abuse of children should not be tolerated in our society.)

7. ✔ The source of Morley Callaghan's title *They Shall Inherit the Earth* is a verse in the New Testament.

8. ✔ The reason she did not come to class is that she was sick.

9. ✔ The beach is the place where I get my worst sunburn.

10. ✔ Honesty is examplified when someone finds a wallet and takes it to the police.

But now we must point out an important exception to the principle of semantic compatibility between the subject and the predicate. Whenever a metaphor is used, there is, in a sense, a semantic incompatibility between the subject and the predicate. On the literal level, it is nonsense to say "That man is a lion in battle," because, strictly speaking, we cannot predicate lionhood of a human being. But we soon develop enough sophistication in language to recognize that in instances like this the predicate term is being used in a transferred or figurative sense. We understand that the man is not being literally equated with a lion—that is, the man is not really a lion; however, he is being compared to a lion—that is, the man has certain ferocious qualities that remind us of a ravaging lion. Recognizing the metaphorical use of the word *lion*, we do not feel that this complement is semantically incompatible with the subject.

Until writers gain the assured familiarity with words that will prevent the choice of the wrong word for what they intend to say, they will have to be cautious in their choice of words, and they may have to consult a dictionary frequently.

22

Choose the precise word for what you want to say.

Examples of imprecise words:

1 **X** I liked the movie *Gone with the Wind* because it was **beautiful.**
2 **X** What most impressed me about the poem was the poet's **descriptive** language.
3 **X** Has-been athletes always have a **sore** look on their face.

Style

4 X To protect her from catching a cold, he insisted that she wear the **gigantic** galoshes.

5 X Honesty is a **thing** that we should value highly.

6 X Jane sold her car, **as** she was planning to take a trip to Europe.

Whereas a "wrong word" misses the target entirely, an "imprecise word" hits all around the bull's-eye but never on dead centre.

☐ The word **beautiful** in example **1** above is too general to convey a precise meaning. The readers' response to a general word like that would be to ask, "In what way was the movie beautiful?" If the writer had said "poignant" or "believable" or "edifying" or "inspiring" or "visually pleasing," readers might want some more particulars, but at least they would have a clearer idea of why the writer liked the movie.

☐ The word **descriptive** in example **2** is too vague. Expressions like "the poet's vivid, sensory diction" or "the poet's simple, concrete words" or "the poet's specific adjectives for indicating colours" would give readers a more exact idea of the kind of descriptive language that impressed the writer of the sentence.

☐ **Sore** in example **3** is ambiguous—that is, it has more than one meaning in the context. In order to convey the notion that the former athletes were disgruntled, the writer should say that "they have an angry look on their face" or simply that "they look angry," but in order to convey the notion that the former athletes exhibited physical discomfort, the writer should say that "they have a painful look on their face"—or in some other way say that their faces reflect their aching wounds.

☐ **Gigantic** in example **4** is hyperbolic, or exaggerated. Unless the hyperbolic **gigantic** was deliberately used for humorous effect, a more proportionate word like *big* or *heavy* or *ungainly* should have been used.

In the spoken medium, we often do not have the leisure to search for the precise word; we utter the first word that offers itself. In response to the question "How did you like him?" we might say, "Oh, I thought he was nice enough." If the people with whom we are speaking are not satisfied by our general word of approval, *nice*, they can ask us to be more specific. In the written medium, however, the situation is quite different: we do have the leisure to search for a precise word, and we are not available to the reader who may want more specific information. While we may be able to get by in the oral medium with a catch-all word like **thing,** as in sample **5**, we should strive for more precision in the written medium and say something like **Honesty is a *virtue* that we should value highly.** Consulting a thesaurus or, better yet, a dictionary that gives the meanings of synonyms will frequently yield the exact word for our intended meaning.

The subordinating conjunction **as** carries a variety of meanings, and it is not always possible to tell from the context which of its many meanings it carries in a particular sentence. In sample sentence **6** above **(Jane sold her car, *as* she was planning to take a trip to Europe),** we cannot tell whether **as** is being used in its sense of "because" or "since" or in its sense of "when" or "while." So we should use the conjunction that exactly expresses our intended meaning; **because** she was planning; **when** she was planning; **while** she was planning. We should reserve the conjunction **as** for those contexts in which there is no possibility of ambiguity, as in sentences like "In that situation, he voted exactly **as** he should have" and "Do **as** I say."

23

Choose words that are appropriate to the context.

Examples of inappropriate words:

1 X Before the unbelieving **orbs** of the other players, he advances his piece on the board, arresting his **manual appendage** only when he sees that he is going to land on Boardwalk.

2 X With **mendacious sangfroid,** he remarked, "You don't have to apologize. I've known lots of people who have done it," and in the same **prevaricating** tone, he **asseverates,** "Virtue is as virtue does."

3 X From our study of human growth and development during the first ten years of life, we know about the incredible strength and resilience of the **kid.**

A word is inappropriate to its context if it does not fit, if it is out of tune with, the subject matter, the occasion, the audience, or the personality of the speaker or writer. It is conspicuous by its inharmonious presence.

No word in isolation can be labelled "inappropriate"; it must be seen in the company of other words before it can be declared "inappropriate." Although one would feel safer in making a judgement if one had a larger context, the boldfaced words in examples **1** and **2** above seem to be inappropriate because they are too elegant or inflated for the subject matter—a game of Monopoly in the first sentence, a reporting of a remark made at a party in the second sentence. There seems to be no good reason for the writer of the first sentence not to use the simpler, less pretentious *eyes* for **orbs** and *hand* for **manual appendage.** There may, however, be certain contexts (occasions, speakers, and audiences) in which the words used in sentence **1** could be considered appropriate. Could you describe such a context?

Young writers consciously striving to enlarge their vocabulary often produce sentences like example **2**. Instead of using a thesaurus to find an accurate or precise word for what they want to say, they use it to find an unusual or a polysyllabic word that will make their prose sound "literary." The one hopeful thing that can be said about such writers is that if they are ambitious enough to want to expand their working vocabulary, they will very soon develop enough sophistication about language to know when it is appropriate, and when it is inappropriate, to use "big words."

The more common fault of inappropriateness, however, is diction that is too colloquial, too slangy, for its formal context. Although there are contexts where the colloquial **kid** would be more appropriate than the word *child*, example **3** seems not to be one of those contexts. There are contexts where slang and even the jargon of particular social groups will be perfectly appropriate, but the slang in sample sentence **3** seems to be out of tune with the subject matter and with the majority of the other words in the sentence.

Since dictionaries, thesauruses, and handbooks will not be of much help in telling a writer when a word is appropriate, the writer will have to rely on the criteria of subject matter, occasion, audience, desired effect, and personality of the author. The writer's "voice" must remain consistent with the overall tone that has been established in a particular piece of writing.

How would you improve the example sentences **1**, **2**, and **3** on page 56?

24

Use the proper idiom.

Examples of lapse of idiom:

1 X Although I agree **to** a few of Socrates' principles, I must disagree **to** many of them.

2 X Conformity has been a common tendency throughout **the** Canadian history.

3 X Blake then **differs** the two introductory pieces by contrasting the simplicity and innocence of the child with the maturity and sophistication of the adult.

4 X Harold and the star quarterback from Victoria Composite High also **compared** in being able to throw a clothesline pass.

5 X It's these special characters and their motives that I intend **on concentrating** in this paper.

6 X Abner had no interest or respect **for** the boy.

To label a locution "unidiomatic" is to indicate that native speakers of the language do not say it that way in any dialect of the language. Unidiomatic expressions are one of the most common weaknesses to be found in the prose of unpractised writers. Why do lapses of idiom occur so frequently? They occur often because many writers have not paid close enough attention—have not attuned their ears—to the way native speakers of the language, including themselves, say something. In trying to express themselves on paper, they put down expressions that they would never use in the spoken medium and that they have never heard any other native speaker use.

No native speaker of the English language, for instance, would use the article **the** in the phrase **throughout the Canadian history** (see example **2** above). However, a North American speaker would say "He was in the hospital," whereas a British speaker would say "He was in hospital." Some Asian speakers have trouble with the English article, because their language does not use a part of speech like our article.

Lapses of idiom frequently occur with prepositions. A number of prepositions fit idiomatically with the verb **agree,** but writers must attune their ears to the proper idiom in the proper place. They can say **agree to** in an expression like "He agreed to the conditions we laid down." They can say **agree on** in an expression like "They can't agree on the wording of the proposal." The preposition that fits idiomatically with the sense of **agree** and **disagree** in example **1** above is **with:** "I agree **with** a few of Socrates' principles" and "I disagree **with** many of them."

Unidiomatic prepositions often appear in compounded phrases, as in example **6**. The preposition **for** does fit with **respect** ("respect for the boy"), but it does not fit with **interest** ("interest for the boy"). In such cases, the idiomatic preposition must be inserted for both members of the compound—e.g., "Abner had no interest **in,** nor respect **for,** the boy."

In phrasing example sentences **3**, **4**, and **5**, native speakers would say "Blake then **differentiates between** the two introductory pieces . . ." and "Harold and the star quarterback from Victoria Composite High were also **comparable** in their ability to throw . . ." and ". . . that I intend to **concentrate on** in this paper."

What prevents a handbook from setting reliable guidelines for proper idioms is the fact that logic plays little or no part in establishing idiom. If logic played such a part, we would say "He looked *down* the word in the dictionary" instead of "He looked *up* the word in the dictionary." Although the eye normally runs down the columns of a dictionary when searching for a word, native speakers say "look up" a word simply because that is the way people have always phrased that locution. Editors or instructors can call your attention to an unidiomatic expression and insert the correct idiom, but they cannot give you any rule that will prevent other lapses of idiom. You simply have to learn proper idioms by reading carefully and by listening intently.

25

Avoid trite expressions.

Examples of trite expressions:

1 **X** I returned from the picnic **tired but happy,** and that night I **slept like a log.**

2 **X** A major objective of high school is to provide a **well-rounded education.**

3 **X** The construction of two new hotels was a **giant step forward** for the community.

4 **X** In the past few years, the popularity of tennis has grown **by leaps and bounds.**

5 **X** Convinced now that drugs are a temptation for young people, the community must **nip the problem in the bud** before it **runs rampant.**

There is nothing grammatically or idiomatically wrong with a trite expression. A trite expression is *stylistically* objectionable—mainly because it is a *tired* expression. Whether or not an expression is "tired" is, of course, a relative matter. What is a cliché for some readers may be bright-penny new for others. But it would be surprising if the expressions in the examples above were not jaded for most readers.

Trite expressions are combinations of words that have been used so often that they have lost their freshness and even their meaning for most readers. Metaphors are especially prone to staleness. Metaphors like "nip in the bud," "slept like a log," "giant step" were once fresh and cogent; they are now wilted.

Overworked combinations like "a well-rounded education" should be banished from the language, partly because they are boring and partly because they no longer convey a precise meaning. Someone should be daring enough to mint the expression "a well-squared education" and see whether it gains currency.

Be wary of weary words.

26

Rephrase awkwardly constructed sentences.

Examples of awkward sentences:

1 X You could get much of the best exercise people could undertake, walking. I believe people should walk at a leisurely pace, with no set goal on distance.

2 X The football player has had many broken noses, with which he ends up looking like a prizefighter.

Style

3 X
I and probably everybody else who started learning to drive in their second year of high school thought the only thing to do was to drive fast so that we could be recognized as the ones who had learned to control our vehicles in difficult situations.

Awkward sentences are sentences so ineptly put together that the resultant jumble of words is difficult to read or understand. An awkward sentence is often the result of a writer's saying something in a wordy, roundabout way rather than in a terse, direct way. The problem is that writers of awkwardly constructed sentences are usually not aware that they have done so; they have to be told that their sentences are awkward.

The ear, however, is a reliable resource for detecting awkward sentences. If writers adopt the practice of reading their sentences aloud, they will often detect clumsy, odd-sounding combinations of words. Alerted by the ear, they should look for the usual causes of awkwardness: **excessive verbiage, words and phrases out of their normal order, successions of prepositional phrases** ("the president of the largest chapter of the national fraternity of students of dentistry"), **split constructions** ("I, chastened by my past experiences, resolved to never consciously and maliciously circulate, even if true, damaging reports about my friends"), **successions of rhyming words** ("He tries wisely to revise the evidence supplied by his eyes"). In their efforts to rephrase sentences, writers should try expressing the same thought in the way they would if they were *speaking* the sentence to someone.

The sample sentences above are awkward for a variety of reasons, but what they all have in common is excessive verbiage. Pruning some of the deadwood, rearranging some of the parts, using simpler, more idiomatic phrases, we can improve the articulation of those clumsy sentences:

1 ✔ Walking is the best exercise. People should walk at a leisurely pace and only as far as they feel like going.

2 ✔ The football player has broken his nose so often that he looks like a prizefighter.

3 ✔ Like others who learned to drive in their second year of high school, I thought that driving fast was the best way to be recognized as a skillful operator.

27

Cut out unnecessary words.

Examples of wordy sentences:

1 X He was justified in trying to straighten out his mother on her backward ideas about her attitude toward Indians. (19 words)

2 X In this modern world of today, we must get an education that will prepare us for a job in our vocation in life. (23 words)

3 X In the "Garden of Love," the poem relates the sad experience of a child being born into a cruel world. (20 words)

4 X The meaning, at least in my own eyes, that he is trying to convey in the poem "Arms and the Boy" is of the evilness of war in that it forces innocent people to take up the instruments of death and destruction and then tries to teach them to love to use them to kill other human beings. (58 words)

5 X These rivers do not contain fish, due to the fact that the flow of water is too rapid. (18 words)

A "wordy sentence" is one in which a writer has used more words than are needed. Writers would soon learn to cultivate restraint if they were charged for every word used, as they

Style

are when sending a telegram. They should not, of course, strive for a "telegraphic" style or a "headline" style, but they should value words so much that they spend them sparingly.

Let us see if we can trim the sample sentences without substantially altering their meaning:

1. ✔ He was justified in trying to straighten out his mother's attitude toward Indians. (13 words)
2. ✔ In the modern world, we must get an education that will prepare us for a job. (16 words)
3. ✔ The "Garden of Love" relates the sad experience of a child being born into a cruel world. (17 words)
4. ✔ As I see it, the poet's thesis in "Arms and the Boy" is that war is evil because it not only forces people to take up arms but makes them use these weapons to kill other human beings. (38 words)
5. ✔ These rivers do not contain fish, because the water flows too rapidly. (12 words)

Notice that each of the revised sentences uses fewer words than the original. The retrenchment ranges from three words to twenty words. If the writers were being charged a quarter a word, they could probably find other superfluous words to prune. The writer of sentence **4**, for instance, would probably lop off **As I see it** and **in "Arms and the Boy,"** and condense **to kill other human beings** to **to kill others.**

One should not become obsessed with saving words, but one should seize every opportunity of clearing out obvious deadwood. As Alexander Pope said,

Words are like leaves, and where they most abound,
Much fruit of sense beneath is rarely found.

28

Avoid careless repetition of words and ideas.

Examples of careless repetition:

1 X Professor Parker, a **fellow colleague,** offered to intercede with the dean.

2 X He does not rely on the **surrounding environment** as much as his brother does.

3 X The objective point of view accentuates the emotional intensity of the love affair and the **impending** failure that will **eventually happen.**

4 X **In Larry's mind** he thinks, "I have never met anyone so absorbed in himself."

5 X There are some striking similarities between Segal and Hemingway, for **both** have studied life and love and found them **both** to be failures.

6 X After **setting** up camp, we **set** off to watch the sun **set**.

A "careless repetition" refers to the needless repetition of a word in the same sentence (or in adjoining sentences) or to the juxtaposition of synonymous words that produces what is called a **redundancy** or a **tautology.**

The repetition of the pronoun **both** in example **5** above is especially careless because the repeated pronouns have different antecedents (the first one refers to **Segal** and **Hemingway,** the second to **life** and **love**). The emphasis in this caution about the repetition of a word should be put on the word *needless*. In sentence **6**, we have an instance of the same basic verb form **(set)** used in three different senses. Unless the writer here was deliberately playing on words, it would have been better to avoid the awkward repetition, saying something like **After preparing camp, we**

Style

went off to watch the sun set. Sometimes it is better to repeat a word, even in the same sentence, than to run the risk of ambiguity or misunderstanding. In a sentence like "She told her mother that her hairdryer was broken," if the ambiguity of the second **her** could not be remedied in some other way, it would be better to repeat the noun—e.g., "She told her **mother** that the **mother's** hairdryer was broken." In this case, however, there is a better way to avoid the ambiguity of the pronoun—namely, by putting the sentence in direct discourse: "She told her mother, 'Your hairdryer is broken' " or "She told her mother, 'My hairdryer is broken.' "

The boldfaced words in examples **1**, **2**, **3**, and **4** are instances of redundancy or tautology (needless repetition of the same idea in different words). **Fellow** and **colleague, surrounding** and **environment, impending** and **eventually happen** are examples of repetitions of the same idea in different words. In examples **1** and **2**, drop the first boldfaced word; in example **3**, drop the whole **that** clause. In example **4**, the phrase **in Larry's mind** is superfluous (where else does one think but in the mind?). Say simply, **Larry thinks, "I have never met anyone so absorbed in himself."**

Repetition of key words can be an effective means of achieving coherence (see **32**, dealing with paragraph coherence, in the next section). What you are here being cautioned about is the redundant and therefore unnecessary expression of words and ideas.

29

Avoid mixed metaphors.

Examples of mixed metaphors:

1 X Sarty finally comes to the point where his inner turmoil reaches its **zenith** and **stagnates in a pool** of lethargy.

2 X In "The Dead," James Joyce uses small talk as an effective **weapon** to **illustrate** his thesis.

3 X He tried to **scale the wall** of indifference between them but found that he couldn't **burrow** through it.

4 X Billy was **living in a dream world** that was **wrapped up in his thoughts.**

☐ A mixed metaphor is the result of a writer's failure to maintain a consistent image. All metaphors are based on the perceived likenesses between two things that exist in a different order of being—as for instance between a *man* and a *greyhound* ("The lean shortstop is a greyhound when he runs the bases"), *fame* and a *spur* ("Fame is the spur to ambition"), *mail* and an *avalanche* ("The mail buried the staff under an avalanche of complaints"). Whenever any detail is incompatible with one or other of the terms of the analogy, the metaphor is said to be "mixed."

Zenith, as in example **1** above, connotes something sky-rocketing, and therefore that detail is incompatible with the detail of stagnation. It is also difficult to reconcile the notion of **turmoil** with a **stagnant pool;** turmoil connotes violent movement, but a pool is static.

A **weapon** is not used to **illustrate** something. If one were climbing **(scaling)** a wall, one could not dig **(burrow)** through it at the same time. In example **4** above, Billy is living *in* a dream world, but that dream world is, in turn, wrapped up in Billy's thoughts.

Forming and maintaining a clear picture of the notion one is attempting to express figuratively will ensure a consistent metaphor.

The following revision of sentence **1** unscrambles the mixed metaphor:

🖝 Sarty finally comes to the point where his turmoil reaches its zenith and fizzles out into lethargy.

Unscramble the metaphors in sentences **2**, **3**, and **4**.

30

Consider whether an active verb would be preferable to a passive verb.

Examples of questionable use of the passive voice:

1 X Money **was borrowed** by the couple so that they could pay off all their bills.

2 X His love for her **is shown** by his accepting her story and by his remaining at her side when she is in trouble.

3 X From these recurrent images of hard, resistant metals, it **can be inferred** by us that he was a mechanical, heartless person.

4 X Talking incessantly, he **was overwhelmed** by the girl.

The passive voice of the verb is a legitimate and useful part of the English language. A sentence using a passive verb as its predicate is a different but synonymous way of expressing the thought conveyed by a sentence using an active verb. The basic formula for a sentence using an active-verb construction is as follows:

NOUN PRASE₁	+	VERB	+	NOUN PHRASE₂

The judge   pronounced   the verdict

The formula for transforming that active-verb construction into a passive-verb construction is as follows:

NOUN PHRASE₂	+	AUXILIARY	+	VERB	+	**by**	+	NOUN PHRASE₁

(past participle form)

The verdict   was   pronounced   by   the judge

Notice the changes that have taken place in the second sentence: (1) Noun Phrase₁ and Noun Phrase₂ have switched positions, and (2) two words have been added, the auxiliary **was** and the preposition **by**. Although the second sentence expresses the same thought as the first sentence, it is longer, by two words, than the first sentence.

If the use of a passive verb is questionable, it is questionable only stylistically; that is, one can question the *choice* of a passive verb rather than an active verb in a particular instance. By questioning the use of the passive verb, the critic is merely asking the writer to consider whether the sentence would not be more emphatic, more economical, less awkward, and somehow "neater" if an active verb were used. Challenged to consider the options available in a particular case, writers still have the privilege of making the choice that seems better to them.

The writers of the sample sentences **1**, **2**, and **3** above should consider whether their sentences would be improved by the use of an active verb, as in these revisions:

Style

1 ✔ The couple **borrowed** money so that they could pay off all their bills.

2 ✔ He **shows** his love for her by accepting her story and by remaining at her side when she is in trouble.

3 ✔ From these recurrent images of hard, resistant metals, we **can infer** that he was a mechanical, heartless person.

The writer of example **1 (Money was borrowed by the couple so that they could pay off all their bills)** might argue that special emphasis had to be placed on **money,** and so **money** was made the subject of the sentence and put in the emphatic lead-off position in the sentence (**money was borrowed** . . .). Writers can also justify use of a passive verb when they do not know the agent of an action or prefer not to reveal the agent or consider it unnecessary to indicate the agent, as in the sentence "The story was reported to all the newspapers."

Dangling verbals often result from the use of a passive-verb construction in the main clause (see **13** on dangling verbals). The writer of sentence **4** in the examples above **(Talking incessantly, he was overwhelmed by the girl)** may not have had a choice. The context of that sentence suggests that the lead-off participial phrase **(talking incessantly)** may be dangling—that is, that it was not the boy **(he)** but the girl who was talking incessantly. If that is the case, the writer may not choose the passive verb instead of the active verb; the active verb *must* be used: **Talking incessantly, the girl overwhelmed him.**

Paragraphing

Introduction

One way to regard paragraphing is to view it as a system of punctuating stages of thought presented in units larger than the word and the sentence. Paragraphing is a means of alerting readers to a shift of focus in the development of the main idea of the discourse. It marks off for the reader's convenience the discrete but related parts of the whole discourse. How paragraphing facilitates reading would be made dramatically evident if a whole discourse were written or printed—as ancient manuscripts once were—in a single, unbroken block.

Like punctuation and mechanics, paragraphing is a feature only of the written language. Some linguists claim that speakers of connected discourse signal their "paragraphs" by pauses and by shifts in the tone of their voice. (The next time you hear a speech being delivered from a written text, see if you can detect when the speaker shifts to another paragraph of the manuscript.) But speakers are not conscious—especially in extemporaneous stretches of talk—of paragraphing the stream of sound as writers must be when they are writing their manuscripts.

The typographical device most commonly used to mark off new paragraphs is *indentation*. The first line of each new

Paragraphing

paragraph starts several spaces (usually five or six spaces on the typewriter) from the left-hand margin. Another convention for marking paragraphs in printed texts is the block system: beginning every line at the left-hand margin but leaving double or triple spacing between paragraphs.

In this section, only three aspects of the paragraph are treated: **unity**, **coherence**, and **adequate development**. The traditional means of developing the central idea of a paragraph are mentioned in the section on adequate development, but they are not discussed at length as they are in most of the rhetoric texts. However, if writers take care of unity, coherence, and adequate development, they will be attending to the three most persistent and common problems that beset the composition of written paragraphs.

31

Preserve the unity of the paragraph.

Examples of paragraphs lacking unity:

1 X The eminence of Samuel Johnson inclines modern scholars to study his thoughts and opinions. His multifarious knowledge intrigued his contemporaries. Although he manifested his interest in the drama by editing Shakespeare, he did not enjoy the theatre. He was envious too of his former pupil David Garrick, the greatest actor of the eighteenth century.

2 X "The Cradle Song" from the *Songs of Innocence* has internal rhyme. In this poem, the child is quiet and happy. It has a heavenly image, and throughout the poem, the mother sheds tears of joy. It has a persona—that is, one who speaks for the poet—who is naive and innocent. The poem "Infant Sorrow" contrasts with "The Cradle Song," and this contrast is very distinct. One can see a screaming and devilish child. The piping is a harsh sound, and the child, who's against restrictions, is looking back and realizing that there is no paradise on earth.

3 X Dr. Rockwell let his feelings be known on only one subject: the administration. He felt that the administrative system was outdated. Abolishing grades, giving the student a voice in administration, and revamping the curriculum were three steps he felt should be taken to improve the system. Dr. Rockwell taught in this manner. In class, a mysterious aura surrounded him. He was aware of what was going on, but he preferred to hear the members of the class rather than himself. He was quiet and somewhat shy. His eyes caught everything that went on in class. His eyes generated a feeling of understanding.

The principle governing paragraph unity is that a paragraph should develop a single topic or thesis, which is often, but not always, announced in a topic sentence. Every sentence in the paragraph should contribute in some way to the development of that single idea. If writers introduce other ideas into the paragraph, they will violate the unity of the paragraph and disorient the reader.

In a sense, all three of the sample paragraphs discuss a single idea or topic: the first one talks about Samuel Johnson; the second one talks about William Blake's poetry; the third one talks about a teacher, Dr. Rockwell. But in another sense, all three paragraphs present a confusing mixture of unrelated ideas.

The first sentence of sample paragraph **1**, which has the air of being a "topic sentence," talks about what Samuel Johnson means to modern scholars. Instead of the second sentence going on to develop that idea, it mentions what Dr. Johnson meant to his contemporaries. The third sentence talks about his attitude toward the drama and the theatre. The fourth sentence mentions his envy of his former pupil

Paragraphing

David Garrick. What we have in this paragraph are four topics. A whole paragraph or a whole paper could be devoted to the development of each of these four topics, but here they are packed into a single paragraph.

We have observed that sample paragraph **2** has a certain unity: each sentence is saying something about a poem by William Blake. But notice that the paragraph talks about *two* poems by Blake. Even though the paragraph is about two poems, we could still detect some unity in the paragraph if we viewed it as developing a contrast between two poems by the same author. But even if we were generous enough to concede that much unity to the paragraph, it would be difficult for us to perceive a unifying theme among the many disparate things said about the two poems.

Sample paragraph **3** also has a certain unity: each sentence in the paragraph is talking about the teacher, Dr. Rockwell. And there is a tight unity in the first three sentences: each of these sentences talks about Dr. Rockwell's attitude toward the administration. But with the fourth sentence of the paragraph, the writer introduces another and unrelated topic: a description of how Dr. Rockwell conducted himself in the classroom. If the writer had broken up this stretch of prose into two paragraphs, each of the two paragraphs would have had its own unity.

3 ✔   Dr. Rockwell let his feelings be known on only one subject: the administration. His estimate of the administrative system of the school was largely negative. He felt, for instance, that the administrative system was outdated. Abolishing grades, giving students a voice in administration, and revamping the curriculum were three steps he felt should be taken to improve the system.

Dr. Rockwell's demeanor in the classroom was remarkable. Although there was a mysterious aura about him, he was always aware of what was going on. His eyes caught everything that went on in class, but they generated a feeling of understanding. Even though he was a very learned scholar, this quiet, somewhat shy man preferred to listen to the members of the class rather than himself.

A paragraph will have unity, will have "oneness," if every sentence in it has an obvious bearing on the development of a single topic. When a new topic is to be introduced, the writer should begin another paragraph.

32

Compose the paragraph so that it reads coherently.

Examples of incoherent paragraphs:

1 X The first stanza of "The Echoing Green" does not correspond with any other poem by Blake. The glory of nature's beauty is presented in vivid details. Emotional intensity is the overall effect of the poem. Blake resents the mechanization which has been brought about by the Industrial Revolution. The rhythm of the verses contributes to the meditative mood.

2 X The preceding account illustrates all the frustrations that a beginning golfer experiences. The dominant philosophy is that the golfer who looks the best plays the best. He complicates the game by insisting on perfection the first time he sets foot on the course. More time and money are spent on clothes and equipment than on the most important aspect, skill. Winning is the only goal. Where is the idea of recreation? Try playing without a caddy sometime, and see how much exercise you get.

3 X After the program has been written, each line is punched onto a card. The deck of cards is known as the "program source deck." The next step is to load the program compiler into the computer. The compiler is a program written in machine language for a particular computer, which reads the source deck and performs a translation of the pro-

Paragraphing

gram language into machine language. The machine language, in the form of instructions, is punched onto cards. This machine-language deck of cards is known as the "object deck." After the object deck has been punched, the programmer is then able to execute his program. The program is run by loading the object deck into the computer. The run of the program marks the end of the second step.

Coherence is that quality which makes it easy for a reader to *follow* a writer's train of thought as it moves from sentence to sentence and from paragraph to paragraph. It facilitates reading because it ensures that the reader will be able to detect the relationships of the parts. It also reflects the clear thinking of the writer because it results from the arrangement of the writer's thoughts in some kind of perceivable order and from the use of those verbal devices that help to stitch thoughts together. In short, as the roots of the Latin word suggest (*co*, "together," + *haerere*, "to stick"), coherence helps the parts of a discourse "stick together."

Here are some ways in which to achieve coherence in a paragraph (not all of these devices, of course, have to be used in every paragraph):

(a) Repeat key words from sentence to sentence or use recognizable synonyms for key words.

(b) Use pronouns for key nouns. (Because a pronoun gets its meaning from the noun to which it refers, it is by its very nature one of those verbal devices that help to stitch sentences together.)

(c) Use demonstrative adjectives, "pointing words" (**this** statement, **that** plan, **these** developments, **those** disasters).

(d) Use conjunctive adverbs, "thought-connecting words" **(however, moreover, also, nevertheless, therefore, thus,**

subsequently, indeed, then, accordingly).

(e) Arrange the sequence of sentences in some kind of perceivable order (for instance, a **time order,** as in a narrative of what happened or in an explanation of how to do something; a **space order,** as in the description of a physical object or a scene; a **logical order,** such as cause to effect, effect to cause, general to particular, particular to general, whole to part, familiar to unfamiliar).

Example paragraph **3** attempts to describe computer programming, a process that most readers would find difficult to follow because it is complicated and unfamiliar. But the process will be doubly baffling to readers if it is not described coherently. What makes this description of computer programming doubly difficult for the reader to follow is that the writer is doing two things at once: (1) designating the chronological sequence of steps in the process, and (2) defining the technical terms used in the description of the process. It would have been better if the writer had devoted one paragraph to defining such terms as **program source deck, compiler, program language, machine language, object deck.** Then he could have devoted another paragraph exclusively to the description of the process of "running a program"—first you do this, then you do that, and after that you do this, etc. In the present paragraph, the reader gets lost because he is kept bouncing back and forth between definition of the terms and description of the process.

The following revision illustrates the way in which example **3** could be written to achieve greater coherence:

3 ✔ Before you can understand the process of "running a program," you need some definitions of technical terms. After the program discussed in the previous paragraph has been written, each line of that program is punched onto an IBM card. The collection of these cards

Paragraphing

is known as the "program source deck." Another set of cards is known as the "compiler." The compiler "reads" the source deck and translates it into machine language. The machine-language deck of cards that results from the operation of the compiler is known as the "object deck."

The first step in the process is to put the program source deck into the computer. Then in order to translate the program language of the source deck into machine language, the compiler set must be inserted. Following that step, the object deck, with its instructions written out in machine language, is put into the computer. Now the program is ready to be "run" through the computer.

It is more difficult to suggest ways of revising the first two sample paragraphs; they are so incoherent that it is almost impossible to discover what the principal points were that the writers wanted to put across in them. If we could confer with the writers and ask what the main idea of each of their paragraphs was, we could then advise them about which of the sentences contribute to the development of that idea (and which sentences have to be dropped because they threaten the unity of the paragraph), about the order of the sentences in the paragraph, and about the verbal devices that would help to knit the sentences together.

Coherence is a difficult writing skill to master, but the writer who has not acquired at least a measure of that skill will continue to be frustrated in trying to communicate with others on paper. The writer must learn how to compose paragraphs so that the sequence of thoughts flows smoothly, easily, and logically from sentence to sentence. Bridges or links must be provided to allow the reader to pass from sentence to sentence without being puzzled about the relationship of what is said in one sentence to what is said in the next sentence. Note how a skillful writer like Thomas Babington

Macaulay stitches his sentences together by repeating key words and by using pronouns, connecting words and phrases, and parallel structures:

> It will be seen that we do not consider Bacon's ingenious analysis of the inductive method as a very useful performance. Bacon was not, as we have already said, the inventor of the inductive method. He was not even the person who first analyzed the inductive method correctly, though he undoubtedly analyzed it more minutely than any who preceded him. He was not the person who first showed that by the inductive method alone new truth could be discovered. But he was the person who first turned the minds of speculative men, long occupied in verbal disputes, to the discovery of a new and useful truth; and by doing so, he at once gave to the inductive method an importance and dignity which had never belonged to it. He was not the maker of that road; he was not the discoverer of that road; he was not the person who first surveyed and mapped that road. But he was the person who first called the public attention to an inexhaustible mine of wealth, which had been utterly neglected and which was accessible by that road alone. By doing so, he caused that road, which had previously been trodden only by peasants and higglers, to be frequented by a higher class of travellers.

Never write a sentence that is not clearly attached to the preceding and following sentences.

33

Paragraphs should be adequately developed.

Examples of inadequately developed paragraphs:

1 **X** Wilfred Owen combines many topics of imagery to get his point across. Most of his imagery is either ironic or sentimental.

2 **X** The young people now growing up in this mechanized society should be made aware of the many dangers of their reckless driving, just

Paragraphing

> as the young people of another generation were cautioned about the dangers of their engaging in indiscriminate hunting. In both cases, responsibility for one's actions is the chief lesson to be taught.

3 X Before we seek answers to those questions, however, we should settle on a definition of the term *illiteracy*. For most people, *illiteracy* signifies the inability to read and write.

Generally, one- and two-sentence paragraphs are not effective, except for purposes of emphasis, transition, or dialogue.

The preceding one-sentence paragraph can be justified on the ground that the writer wanted to give special emphasis to a principle by setting it aside in a paragraph by itself. Separate paragraphing for emphasis is a graphic device comparable to italicizing (underlining) a word or a phrase in a sentence for emphasis. Set aside in a paragraph by itself, an important idea achieves a prominence that would be missed if the idea were merged with other ideas in the same paragraph.

A one- or two-sentence paragraph can also be used to mark or announce a transition from one major division of a discourse to the next major division. Transitional paragraphs facilitate reading because they orient readers, reminding them of what has been discussed and alerting them to what is going to be discussed. They are like signposts marking the major stages of a journey. Note how the following two-sentence paragraph helps to orient readers:

> After presenting his introduction to *Songs of Experience*, William Blake apparently feels that his readers have been sufficiently warned about their earthly predicament. Let us see how he uses the poems in *Songs of Experience* to illustrate what the people might do to solve their problems.

33 Adequate Development

One of the conventions in printing is that in representing dialogue in a story we should begin a new paragraph every time the speaker changes. A paragraph of dialogue can be one sentence long or ten sentences long (any number of sentences really). A paragraph of dialogue may also consist of only a phrase or a single word:

"It's a beautiful day, isn't it?" Melvin asked.
"Yup," Hank muttered.
"Remember yesterday?"
"Yup."
"I thought it would never stop raining."
"Me too."

Once an exchange like that gets going, the author can dispense with the identifying tags, because the separate paragraphing will mark the shift in speakers.

But except for the purposes of emphasis, transition, or dialogue, a one- or a two-sentence paragraph can rarely be justified; it is almost a contradiction in terms. There can be little if any development in a single sentence. In a two-sentence paragraph, one of the sentences is likely to be the topic sentence; the remaining sentence is hardly enough to develop the topic idea adequately.

Judgment about whether a paragraph is adequately developed is, of course, a relative matter. Because some ideas need more development than others, no one can say absolutely how many sentences a paragraph needs to be satisfactorily developed. But a topic sentence does set at least a general commitment that a writer must fulfill. When the writer of sample paragraph **1** says, in what is obviously the topic sentence, **Wilfred Owen combines many types of imagery to get his point across,** we have every right to

Paragraphing

expect that he or she will specify and discuss several, if not many, types of imagery. But when that topic idea is developed with only one sentence, which is only slightly less general than the first sentence, we can feel quite safe in saying that *this* paragraph is inadequately developed. An obvious way for the writer to develop the ideas contained in the two sentences is to cite examples, first of ironic imagery, then of sentimental imagery. To flesh out the mere cataloguing of these examples, the writer could go on to show how these images help the author "get his point across."

Even if sample paragraph **2** were a summary paragraph that followed a paragraph (or several paragraphs) in which the writer had discussed the disadvantages of indulging in reckless driving, the reader could reasonably expect the writer to say something more about the notion presented in the second sentence. What kind of legal or moral responsibilities do reckless drivers have to themselves? What kind of responsibilities do they have to their families and to society in general? What are the consequences, for themselves and for society, of their refusing to be responsible for their actions? These questions suggest ways in which the writer might have expanded this thinly developed paragraph.

A topic sentence will suggest how long a paragraph has to be in order to create an impression of being adequately developed. Some sentences commit a writer to more development than others. A sentence like "There was only one way in which Julie could rouse John out of bed in the morning" obviously entails less development than a sentence like "There were several ways in which Julie could rouse John out of bed in the morning." Writers must train themselves to look at a topic sentence and see what it commits them to do in the paragraph. Then of course they must have resources at their command to be able to fulfil this commitment. Sometimes they can draw on examples or illustrations to expand their paragraph; sometimes they can develop the topic idea by stating it in a variety of different ways; sometimes they can expand the paragraph by comparison or contrast or by analogy or by an anecdote; or they can trace out the causes or the consequences of what they are talking about. Invention, discovering something to say, is of course the crucial part of the composition process. Thinly developed paragraphs are the result of writers not thinking enough about their subject to discover what they already know about it and what they need to find out about it in order to develop it. Almost invariably they know more about the idea stated in a topic sentence than they put down in a one- or two-sentence paragraph. They must be made aware, or must force themselves to become aware, of all that they really know about the topic idea.

Here is a list of the common ways in which writers develop their paragraphs:

(a) They present examples or illustrations of what they are discussing.

(b) They cite data—facts, statistics, evidence, details, precedents—that corroborate or confirm what they are discussing.

(c) They quote, paraphrase, or summarize the testimony of others about what they are discussing.

(d) They relate an anecdote or event that has some bearing on what they are discussing.

(e) They define terms connected with what they are discussing.

Paragraphing

(f) They compare or contrast what they are discussing with something else—usually something familiar to the readers—and point out similarities or differences.

(g) They explore the causes or reasons for the phenomenon or situation they are discussing.

(h) They point out the effects or consequences of the phenomenon or situation they are discussing.

(i) They explain how something operates.

(j) They describe the person, place, or thing they are discussing.

Using one or other of these means of development, we could expand the inadequately developed sample paragraphs. For example, paragraph **3** is more adequately developed by defining or explaining a key term.

3 ✔ Before we seek answers to those questions, however, we should settle on a definition of the term *illiteracy*. For most people, *illiteracy* signifies a person's inability to read and write. But that general definition does not reveal the wide range of disabilities covered by the term. There are those who cannot read or write anything in their native language. Others can read minimally, but they cannot write anything— not even their own name. A large number of people have minimal skills in reading and writing, but they cannot apply those skills to some of the ordinary tasks of day-to-day living—for example, they cannot make sense of the written instructions on a can of weed-killer or fill out an application form. Such people are sometimes referred to as being "functionally illiterate." So whenever we discuss the problem of illiteracy with others, we should make sure what degree of disability people have in mind when they use the term *illiteracy*. *(expanded by defining or explaining a key term)*

Punctuation

Introduction

Graphic punctuation, which is the only kind dealt with in this section, is a feature of the written language exclusively. For the written language, it performs the kinds of functions that intonation (pitch, stress, pause, and juncture) performs for the spoken language. Punctuation and intonation can be considered as part of the grammar of a language because they join with other grammatical devices (word order, inflections, and function words) to help convey meaning. If writers would regard punctuation as an integral—and often indispensable—part of the expressive system of a language, they might cease to think of it as just another nuisance imposed on them by editors and English teachers.

In *Structural Essentials of English* (New York: Harcourt Brace Jovanovich, 1956), Harold Whitehall has neatly summarized the four main functions of graphic punctuation:

☐ For LINKING parts of sentences and words.
   semicolon
   colon
   dash
   hyphen (for words only)

Punctuation

☐ For SEPARATING sentences and parts of sentences.
period
question mark
exclamation mark
comma

☐ For ENCLOSING parts of sentences.
pair of commas
pair of dashes
pair of parentheses
pair of brackets
pair of quotation marks

☐ For INDICATING omissions.
apostrophe (e.g. **don't, we'll, it's, we've**)
period (e.g. abbreviations, **Mrs., U.S., A.H. Robinson**)
dash (e.g., **John R--, D--n!**)
triple periods (. . . to indicate omitted words in a quotation)

Punctuation is strictly a convention. There is no reason in the nature of things why the mark **?** should be used in English to indicate a question. The Greek language, for instance, uses **;** (what we call a semicolon) to mark questions. Nor is there any reason in the nature of things why the single comma should be a separating device rather than a linking device. Usage has established the distinctive functions of the various marks of punctuation. And although styles of punctuation have changed somewhat from century to century and even from country to country, the conventions of punctuation set forth in the following section are the prevailing conventions in North America in the second half of the twentieth century. Although publishers of newspapers, magazines, and books often have style manuals that prescribe, for their own editors and writers, a style of punctuation that may differ in some particulars from the prevailing conventions, writers who observe the conventions of punctuation set forth in this section can rest assured that they are following the predominant system in North America.

34

Put a comma in front of the co-ordinating conjunction that joins the independent clauses of a compound sentence.

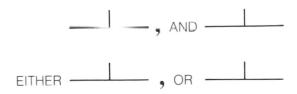

Examples:

1 ✔ He disliked this kind of cruel humour **,** yet when he met the actress at a dinner party, he teased her unmercifully.

2 ✔ Alice's embarrassment amused Bill **,** so he deliberately pursued the conversation with the old man.

3 ✔ The decision about whether to attend college should be left entirely to the child **,** and the parents should make every effort to reconcile themselves to the child's decision.

4 ✔ It was snowing outside **,** and in the building William felt safe.

5 ✔ Nick relates all the happenings in his own words **,** and sometimes his own interpretations of another character or situation are revealed.

6 ✔ Either the members will reject the proposal **,** or they will modify it in such a way as to make it innocuous.

Punctuation

Pairs of independent clauses joined by one of the co-ordinating conjunctions **(and, but, or, nor, for, yet, so)** or by one of the correlative conjunctions **(either . . . or, neither . . . nor, not only . . . but)** are the only co-ordinate pairs that should be separated with a comma (see **36**). The reason why this convention developed is that in many situations, the absence of the comma could lead to an initial misreading of the sentence, as in example **3** or in a sentence like this: "He returned the book for his mother refused to pay any more fines." In the latter sentence, it would be quite natural for us to read **for** as a preposition. Consequently, we might initially read the sentence this way: **He returned the book for his mother** . . . but when we came to the verb **refused,** we would realize that we had misread the syntax of the sentence and would have to back up and reread the sentence. If you read sample sentences **3**, **4**, and **5** *without the comma,* you will be aware of the possibility of a misreading of those sentences. A comma placed before the co-ordinating conjunction that joins the two parts of a compound sentence will prevent such misreadings.

Some handbooks also authorize you to omit this separating comma if three conditions prevail: (1) if the two clauses of the compound sentence are short, (2) if there is no punctuation within either of the two clauses, and (3) if there is no chance that the syntax will be misread. (The following sentence satisfies these three condiitons: "He said he would go and he did.") However, if you *invariably* insert a comma before the co-ordinating conjunction that joins the independent clauses of a compound sentence, you never have to pause to consider whether there is a chance that your sentence will be misread, and you can be confident that your sentence will always be read correctly the first time.

35

Introductory words, phrases, or clauses should be separated from the main (independent) clause by a comma.

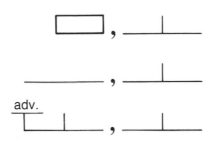

Examples:

1 ✔Underneath **,** the papers were scorched.
(introductory word)

2 ✔I tiptoed into the house. Inside **,** the front room looked as though it had been recently finger-painted by a group of three-year-olds.
(introductory word)

3 ✔In addition to the logical errors **,** Doris had made several miscalculations in addition and subtraction.
(introductory prepositional phrase)

4 ✔As we went by **,** the wharf appeared around the curve.
(introductory adverb clause)

5 ✔After hurriedly gathering **,** the crowd decided to rush the gates.
(introductory verbal phrase)

6 ✔Although he vehemently protested **,** the violence was not as destructive as he predicted it would be.
(introductory adverb clause)

Punctuation

The reason this convention developed is that the comma facilitates the reading of the sentence and often prevents an initial misreading. Without the "protective" comma in the six examples above, the syntax of those sentences would probably be misread on the first reading. If the comma were left out, most readers would probably read the sentences in this way:

1 Underneath the papers... .
2 Inside the front room... .
3 In addition to the logical errors [that] Doris had made... .
4 As we went by the wharf... .
5 After hurriedly gathering the crowd... .
6 Although he vehemently protested the violence... .

The insertion of a comma after the introductory element prevents that kind of misreading.

Even in those instances, however, where there is little or no chance of an initial misreading, the insertion of a comma after the introductory word, phrase, or clause will facilitate the reading of the sentence. Put a comma after the introductory word, phrase, or clause, in the following sentences, and see whether it isn't easier to read the sentences:

Besides the crowd wasn't impressed by his flaming oratory.

Having failed to impress the crowd with his flaming oratory he tried another tactic.

After he saw that his flaming oratory had not impressed the crowd he tried another tactic.

If writers *always* insert a comma after an introductory word, phrase, or clause, they will not have to consider each time whether it would be safe to omit the comma, and they can be confident that their sentences will not be misread.

36

Pairs of words, phrases, or dependent clauses joined by one of the co-ordinating conjunctions should not be separated with a comma.

Examples:

1 ✔ The **mother AND** the **father appeared** in court **AND testified** about their son's activities.
   *(two nouns and two verbs joined by **and**)*

2 ✔ There was nothing they could do **to prevent** the gas attack **NOR to protect** themselves against the gas once it had been released.
   *(two infinitive phrases joined by **nor**)*

3 ✔ The men **who are able to work BUT who are not willing to work** will not be eligible to receive unemployment insurance payments.
   *(two adjective clauses joined by **but**)*

The principle behind this convention is that what has been joined by one means (the co-ordinating conjunction) should not then be separated by another means (the comma, a separating device). The function of the co-ordinating conjunction is to join units of equal rank (e.g., nouns with nouns, verbs with verbs, prepositional phrases with prepositional phrases, participial phrases with participial phrases, adjective clauses with adjective clauses, adverb clauses with

Punctuation

adverb clauses). Once pairs of co-ordinate units have been joined by the conjunction, it makes no sense to separate them with a comma, like this: **the mother, and the father.** If a co-ordinating conjunction is not used to join the pair, a comma should be used to separate the pair, like this: "the tall, handsome man" (but not "the tall, and handsome man").

One exception to this convention, as in **34**, is a pair of *independent* clauses joined by a co-ordinating conjunction. According to **34**, a comma should be inserted before the co-ordinating conjunction, because in this particular structure the omission of the comma could lead—and often does lead—to an initial misreading of the sentence. But there are almost no instances where the use of a comma would prevent the misreading of pairs of words, phrases, or dependent clauses joined by a co-ordinating conjunction. As a matter of fact, if sample sentence **1** were punctuated in this fashion, it would be harder to read: **The mother, and the father appeared in court, and testified about the son's activities.** If some subtle distinction in meaning were effected by these commas, or if the clarity of the sentence were threatened by the absence of the commas, the writer might be able to justify the use of commas in this sentence; but neither of those conditions seems to prevail here. The commas would only confuse the reader.

An exception to this convention occurs in the case of suspended structures, as in the following sentence:

This account of an author's struggles with, and his anxieties about, his writing fascinated me.

36 Pairs (No Comma)

The phrases *struggles with* and *anxieties about* are called "suspended structures" because they are left "hanging" until the noun phrase *his writing,* which completes them grammatically, occurs. If this sentence could have been written "This account of an author's struggles and anxieties about his writing fascinated me," the writer would not, in accord with the directions in **36**, have put a comma in front of the *and* that joins the pair of nouns *struggles* and *anxieties*. But the writer saw that although the preposition *about* fitted idiomatically with *anxieties,* it did not fit idiomatically with *struggles*. So the writer was faced with two choices. Both structures could be completed: "This account of an author's struggles with his writing and his anxieties about his writing fascinated me." But preferring to avoid the repetition of *his writing,* the writer chose to use suspended structures, and alerted the reader to the suspended structures by putting a comma after *with* and after *about.* Inserting a comma before the conjunction *and,* which joins the two phrases, makes it easier for us to read the sentence.

Unless you have some compelling reason, like protecting the clarity of the sentence or facilitating the reading of a sentence, do not separate with a comma pairs of parallel elements that have been joined with a co-ordinating conjunction.

Punctuation

37

Use a comma to separate a series of co-ordinate words, phrases, or clauses.

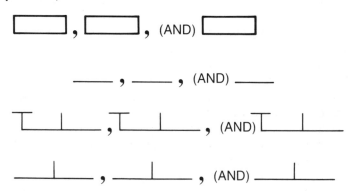

(The parentheses around **and** in the diagrams above indicate that the co-ordinating conjunction between the last two members of a series may sometimes be dispensed with. For instance, the phrasing **The tall, robust, gray-haired soldier rose to speak** is stylistically preferable to **The tall, robust, and gray-haired soldier rose to speak**.)

Examples:

1 ✓ Could he cope with the challenges posed by war, poverty, pollution, and crime?
   (a series of nouns)

2 ✓ He would have to terminate the war, alleviate the plight of the poor, arrest the contamination of the environment, and hobble the criminal.
   *(series of infinitive phrases, with **to** understood in the last three members of the series)*

3 🖊 If he is willing to work hard, if he is resourceful enough to formulate sensible policies, if he subordinates his own interests to the interests of the community, he could rescue the nation from the despair that now prevails.
(series of adverb clauses)

Whereas the convention stated in **36** says that *pairs* of co-ordinate words, phrases, or clauses should not be separated with a comma, the convention governing a *series* of co-ordinate words, phrases, or clauses says that these units should be separated with a comma. (A **series** is to be understood as a sequence of **three or more** co-ordinate units.) Built on the principle of parallelism (see **15**), the series always involves words, phrases, or clauses of a similar kind. So a series should never couple nouns with adjectives, prepositional phrases with infinitive phrases, adjective clauses with adverb clauses, etc.

The convention that will be recommended here follows this formula: **a, b, and c.** Another acceptable formula for the series is **a, b and c**—where no comma is used between the last two members of the series when they are joined by a co-ordinating conjunction. The formula **a, b, and c** is adopted here because the alternative formula **(a, b and c)** sometimes leads to ambiguity. Consider the following example, which uses the **a, b and c** formula:

Please send me a gross each of **the red, green, blue, orange and black ties.**

The shipping clerk who received that order might wonder whether five gross of ties (red, green, blue, orange, black) were being ordered or only four gross (red, green, blue, orange-and-black). If five gross were being ordered, a comma after **orange** would specify the order unequivocally; if four

Punctuation

gross were being ordered, hyphens should have been used to signify the combination of colours.

A more common instance of the ambiguity sometimes created by the use of the **a, b and c** formula is one like the following:

> She appealed to **the administrators, the deans and the chairpersons.**

In this sentence, it is not clear whether <u>she</u> appealed to three different groups (administrators, deans, chairpersons—a meaning that would have been clearly indicated by the **a, b, and c** formula) or to only one group, **administrators,** who are then specified in the double appositive **deans and chairpersons.**

Since there is never any chance of ambiguity if you use the **a, b, and c** formula, you would be well advised to adopt this option for punctuating a series.

38

Non-restrictive adjective clauses should be enclosed with a pair of commas.

Examples:

1. ✔ My oldest brother **, who is a chemist ,** was hurt in an accident last week.
2. ✔ The shopkeeper caters only to American tourists **, who usually have enough money to buy what they want ,** and to aristocratic families.

3 ✔ Mordecai Richler's novel**,** **which has been made into a movie,** takes place in the neighbourhood where the author grew up.

4 ✔ The townspeople threaten the strangers**,** **who are looking at the young girl.**

A non-restrictive adjective clause is one that supplies information about the noun that it modifies but information that is not needed to identify the particular person, place, or thing that is being talked about. (The four **that** clauses in the previous sentence, for instance, are **restrictive** adjective clauses—clauses that identify the nouns that they modify.)

In the case of example **1** above, the adjective clause **who is a chemist** supplies additional information about **my oldest brother,** but this information is not needed to identify which of the brothers was hurt in the accident, because the adjective **oldest** sufficiently identifies the brother being talked about.

One test to determine whether an adjective clause is non-restrictive or not is to read the sentence without the adjective clause, and if the particular person, place, or thing being talked about is sufficiently identified by what is left, the adjective clause can be considered non-restrictive—and, according to the convention, should be marked off with enclosing commas. If, for instance, you were to drop the adjective clause from the first example and say **My oldest brother was hurt in an accident last week,** your readers would not have to ask, "Which one of your brothers was hurt?" The brother is specified by the adjective **oldest,** since there can be only one oldest brother. The clause **who is a chemist** merely supplies some additional but non-essential information about the oldest brother.

Punctuation

Another test to determine whether an adjective clause is non-restrictive or not is the **intonation** test. Read these two sentences aloud:

> He caters to American tourists, who have enough money to buy what they want, and to aristocratic families.
>
> He caters to American tourists who have enough money to buy what they want and to aristocratic families.

In reading the first sentence aloud, native speakers of the language would pause briefly after the words **tourists** and **want** (that is, in the places where the commas are in the written form of the sentence) and would lower the pitch of their voices slightly in enunciating the clause **who have enough money to buy what they want.** In reading the second sentence aloud, native speakers would read right through without a pause and would not lower the pitch of their voices in reading the adjective clause. In writing, it makes a *significant* difference whether the adjective clause in that sentence is or is not enclosed with commas. With the enclosing commas, the sentence means this: He caters to American tourists (who, incidentally, usually have enough money to buy what they want) and to aristocratic families. Without the enclosing commas, the sentence means this: He caters only to those American tourists who have enough money to buy what they want (he doesn't cater to American tourists who don't have enough money to buy) and to aristocratic families. Likewise, the presence of the comma before the adjective clause in example **4** indicates that the townsmen threaten *all* the strangers, because all of them are looking at the young girl. Without the comma before the **who** clause, the sentence would mean that the townspeople threaten *only* those strangers who are looking at the young girl. So whether the adjective clause is marked off with commas or not makes a real difference in the *meaning* of the sentence.

There are some instances in which the adjective clause is almost invariably non-restrictive:

(a) Where the antecedent is a **proper noun,** the adjective clause is usually non-restrictive:

Bob Cratchit, who is a character in Dickens' novel,... .
Montreal, which is on an island in the St. Lawrence,... .
The University of Alberta, which was founded in 1907,... .

(b) Where, in the nature of things, there could be **only one such** person, place, or thing, the adjective clause is usually non-restrictive:

My mother, who is now forty-six years old,... .
Their birthplace, which is Vancouver,...
His fingerprints, which are on file in Ottawa,... .

(c) Where the identity of the antecedent has been clearly established by the **previous context,** the adjective clause is usually non-restrictive:

My brother, who has hazel eyes,...(where it is clear from the context that you have only one brother)

The book, which never made the bestseller list,...(where the previous sentence has identified the particular book being talked about)

Such revolutions, which never enlist the sympathies of the majority of the people,...(where the kinds of revolutions being talked about have been specified in the previous sentences or paragraphs).

Which is the usual relative pronoun that introduces non-restrictive adjective clauses. **That** is the more common relative pronoun used in restrictive adjective clauses. **Who**

Punctuation

(or its inflected forms **whose** and **whom**) is the usual relative pronoun when the antecedent is a person; **that,** however, may also be used when the antecedent is a person and the clause is restrictive: either "the men whom I admire" or "the men that I admire."

39

Restrictive adjective clauses should not be marked off with a pair of commas.

$$\text{(NO COMMA)} \quad \overset{\text{adj.}}{\underline{\qquad \qquad}} \quad \text{(NO COMMA)}$$

Examples:

1 ✔ My brother **who graduated from college in June** was hurt in an accident last week.
2 ✔ The poem is about a boy **who has been in England and has rejoined his family.**
3 ✔ The city is obliged to maintain all streets, alleys, and thoroughfares **that are in the public domain.**

A restrictive adjective clause is one that identifies the particular person, place, or thing being talked about. It "restricts" the noun that it modifies; it "defines"—that is, "draws boundaries around"—the noun being talked about.

In the first example above, the adjective clause **who graduated from college in June** is restrictive because it identifies, defines, designates, specifies which one of the brothers was hurt in the accident. Unlike the non-restrictive adjective clause (see **38**), which merely supplies additional but non-essential information about the noun that it modifies, the restrictive adjective clause supplies information that is needed to identify the noun being talked about.

Whether an adjective clause is restrictive or non-restrictive makes a substantial difference in the meaning of a sentence. Consider, for instance, these two sentences:

People who have unusually slow reflexes should be denied a driver's licence.
(restrictive—note the absence of enclosing commas around the **who** *clause)*

People, who have unusually slow reflexes, should be denied a driver's licence.
(non-restrictive—note the enclosing commas around the **who** *clause)*

The import of the first sentence is that only those people who have unusually slow reflexes should be denied a driver's licence. The import of the second sentence is that *all* people should be denied a driver's licence, because they have unusually slow reflexes. The presence or absence of commas makes a vital difference in the meaning of the two sentences. For this reason, the punctuation of the sentences is not a matter of option or whim.

If you were speaking those two sentences aloud, your voice would do what the presence or the absence of commas does. In the first sentence, your voice would join the **who** clause with **people** by running through without a pause after **people.** In the second sentence, your voice would pause slightly after **people** and would utter the **who** clause on a slightly lower pitch than the rest of the sentence. In addition to the test of whether the adjective clause is needed

Punctuation

to specify the noun referred to, you can use this test of intonation to discriminate restrictive and non-restrictive clauses.

Restrictive adjective clauses modifying non-human nouns should be introduced with the relative pronoun **that** rather than with **which:**

> Governments, which are instituted to protect the rights of people, should be responsive to the will of the people.
> *(non-restrictive)*

> Governments that want to remain in favour with their constituents must be responsive to the will of the people.
> *(restrictive)*

Here is another distinctive fact about the phrasing of restrictive and non-restrictive adjective clauses: the relative pronoun may sometimes be omitted in restrictive clauses, but it may never be omitted in non-restrictive clauses. Note that it is impossible in English to drop the relative pronouns **who** and **whom** from the following non-restrictive clauses:

> John, who is my dearest friend, won't dance with me.

> Marta, whom I love dearly, hardly notices me.

(In the first sentence, however, the clause **who is my dearest friend** could be reduced to an appositive phrase: **John, my dearest friend, won't dance with me.**)

In restrictive adjective clauses, we sometimes have the option of using or not using the relative pronoun:

> The man whom I supported was finally elected.
> *(with the relative pronoun)*

> The man that I supported was finally elected.
> *(with the relative pronoun)*

> The man I supported was finally elected.
> *(without the relative pronoun)*

40 Semicolon, Compound Sentence

In restrictive adjective clauses like these, where the relative pronoun serves as the object of the verb of the adjective clause, the relative pronoun may be omitted. The relative pronoun in restrictive clauses may also be omitted if it serves as the object of a preposition in the adjective clause: "The man I gave the wallet to disappeared" (here the understood **whom** or **that** serves as the object of the preposition **to**). However, the relative pronoun may *not* be omitted when the relative pronoun serves as the subject of the adjective clause:

> Those who exalt themselves shall be humbled.
> *(**who** cannot be omitted)*
> The money that was set aside for scholarships was squandered on roads.
> *(**that** cannot bo omitted)*

40

If the independent clauses of a compound sentence are not joined by one of the co-ordinating conjunctions, they should be joined by a semicolon.

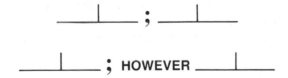

Examples:

1 ✔ This refutation is based on an appeal to reason; however, one must remember that an emotional appeal can also move people to reject an argument.

Punctuation

2 ✔ All the students spontaneously supported the team **;** they wanted to show their loyalty, even though they were disappointed with the outcome of the game.

3 ✔ He loved his mother **;** in fact, he practically worshipped her.

The co-ordinating conjunctions are **and, but, or, nor, for, yet, so.** In the absence of one of those words, the independent clauses of a compound sentence should be spliced together with a punctuation device: the semicolon.

Words and expressions like **however, therefore, then, in fact, on the other hand, on the contrary** are not co-ordinating conjunctions; they are called **conjunctive adverbs.** Conjunctive adverbs provide logical links between sentences and between parts of sentences, but they do not function as grammatical splicers. Unlike co-ordinating conjunctions, which must always be placed *between* the two elements they join, conjunctive adverbs enjoy some freedom of movement in the sentence. In sample sentence **1** above, the word **however** is placed between the two independent clauses, but evidence that this conjunctive adverb is not serving as the grammatical splicer of the two clauses is provided by the fact that **however** can be shifted to another position in the sentence: **This refutation is based on an appeal to reason; one must remember, however, that an emotional appeal can also move people to reject an argument.** The co-ordinating conjunction **but,** on the other hand, could occupy no other position in the sentence than *between* the end of the first clause and the beginning of the next clause.

Nor can the independent clauses of a compound sentence be joined by a comma, because the comma is a

40 Semicolon, Compound Sentence

separating device, not a joining device. Compound sentences so punctuated are called **comma splices** (see **18**). As indicated in **34**, if a compound sentence is joined by one of the co-ordinating conjunctions, a comma should be put in front of the conjunction to mark off the end of one independent clause and the beginning of the next independent clause. But when a co-ordinating conjunction is not present to join the independent clauses, a semicolon must be used to join them. The semicolon serves both to mark the division between the two clauses and to join them.

It is sometimes advisable to use both a semicolon and a co-ordinating conjunction to join the independent clauses of a compound sentence. When the clauses are unusually long and have commas within them, a semicolon placed before the co-ordinating conjunction helps to demarcate the end of one clause and the beginning of the next one, as in this example:

> Struggling to salvage what was left of the semester, he pleaded with his English teacher, who was notoriously softhearted, to grant him an extension of time on his written assignments, quizzes, and class reports**;** **but** he forgot that, even with the best of intentions, he had only so many hours every day when he could study and only a limited reserve of energy.

The co-ordinating conjunction **but** serves to join the two main clauses of the compound sentence, but the use of the semicolon in addition to the conjunction makes it easier to read the sentence.

Punctuation

41

Whenever you use a semicolon, be sure that you have an independent clause on both sides of the semicolon.

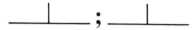

Examples of failure to observe this convention:

1 X He played the banjo expertly **;** although he couldn't read a note of music.

2 X Canadians spend far too many hours as spectators of sports instead of as participants in them **;** watching meaningless drivel on television instead of devoting that time to physical activity.

3 X The two series of poems also differ in style **;** the *Songs of Experience* being more vague and complex than the *Songs of Innocence*.

4 X An industry like this benefits everyone, from the poor, for whom it creates employment **;** to the rich, who are made richer by it.

This convention is the corollary of **40**. It cautions against using the semicolon to join elements of unequal rank.

In all of the examples above, a semicolon has been used to join units of unequal rank. In all these sentences, there is an independent clause on the *left-hand* side of the semicolon; however, there is no independent clause on the *right-hand* side of the semicolon in any of those sentences.

41 Independent Clause Both Sides of Semicolon

In example **1**, there is the independent clause **He played the banjo expertly** on the left-hand side of the semicolon, but on the right-hand side of the semicolon, there is only the adverb clause **although he couldn't read a note of music.** That adverb clause belongs with, depends on, the first clause. Since it is an integral part of the first clause, it should be joined with that clause. The effect of the semicolon is to make the adverb clause part of a new clause that begins after the semicolon. But on the right-hand side of the semicolon, there is no independent clause that the subordinate, dependent adverb clause can be a part of.

Examples **1**, **3**, and **4** can be revised by simply replacing the semicolon with a comma. Example **2**, however, cannot be revised by a simple change of punctuation. The writer has to supply an independent clause after the semicolon. That independent clause can be supplied by adding the words **they spend far too many hours,** so that the whole clause reads, **they spend far too many hours watching meaningless drivel on television instead of devoting that time to physical activity.** So revised, the sentence has an independent clause on *both* sides of the semicolon.

Like the co-ordinating conjunction, for which it can serve as a substitute, the semicolon joins parts of equal rank. Therefore, if there is an independent clause on one side of the semicolon, there must be a balancing independent clause on the other side.

Punctuation

42

Use a colon after a grammatically complete lead-in sentence that formally announces a subsequent enumeration, explanation, illustration, or extended quotation.

Examples:

1 ✔ The courses I am taking this term are as follows: English, sociology, economics, chemistry, and mathematics.

2 ✔ His approach works like this: after displaying his product and extolling its virtues, he asks the homeowner if there is a small rug in the house that should be cleaned.

3 ✔ Examples of the diction used to evoke the horror of the scene include vivid images like these: "coughing like hags," "thick green light," "guttering," "white eyes writhing in his face," "gargling from froth-corrupted lungs."

4 ✔ The reaction of the crowd signified only one thing: apathy.

5 ✔ *(note the use of a colon after a lead-in sentence for an extended quotation in a research paper.)*

Toward the end of the *Preface,* Dr. Johnson confessed that he abandoned his earlier expectation that his dictionary would be able to "fix the language":

Those who have been persuaded to think well of my design will require that it should fix our language and put a stop to those alterations which time and chance have hitherto been suffered to make in it without opposition. With this consequence I will confess that I flattered myself for a while; but now begin to fear that I have indulged expectation which neither reason nor experience can justify.

Note that although a word, a phrase, or a clause or a series of words, phrases, or clauses can follow the colon, there must be an independent clause (a grammatically complete sentence) on the left-hand side of the colon.

In accord with this principle, you should not punctuate a sentence in this fashion:

X The courses I am taking this term are: English, sociology, economics, chemistry, and mathematics.

That punctuation makes no more sense than punctuating a sentence in this way:

X My name is: Paul Johnson.

In both cases, the words following the colon are needed to complete the sentence grammatically.

What distinguishes the colon from the dash as a symbolic device is that the colon throws the reader's attention *forward,* whereas the dash as a linking device throws the reader's attention *backward*. What the colon signifies is that what *follows* is a specification of what was formally announced in the clause on the left-hand side of the colon.

43

Use a dash when the word or word-group that follows it constitutes a summation, an amplification, or a reversal of what went before it.

Examples:

1 ✔ English, psychology, history, and French— —these were the courses I took last term.

Punctuation

2 ✔ If he was pressured, he would become sullen and close-lipped——a reaction that did not endear him to the judge or to the lawyer.

3 ✔ Time and time again he would admit that his critics were right, that he should have realized his mistakes, that he should have read the danger signs more accurately——and then go ahead with his original plans.

Unlike the colon, which directs the reader's attention forward, the dash usually directs the reader's attention backward. What follows the dash, when it is used as a linking device, looks back to what preceded it for the particulars or details that spell out its meaning or invest its meaning with pungency or irony.

The colon and the dash are usually not interchangeable marks of punctuation. They signal a different relationship between the word-groups that precede them and those that follow them. After much practice in writing, one develops a sense for the subtle distinction in relationships that is signalled by the punctuation in the following sentences:

(a) The reaction of the crowd signified only one thing: apathy.

(b) The crowd clearly indicated their indifference to the provocative speech—an apathy that later came back to haunt them.

In sentence **(a)**, the lead-in clause before the colon clearly alerts the reader to expect a specification of what is hinted at in that clause. In sentence **(b)**, there is no such alerting of the reader in the lead-in clause; but following the dash, there is an unexpected commentary on what was said in the lead-in clause, a summary commentary that forces the reader to look backward. The colon and the single dash are both

44 Pair of Dashes, for Parenthetical Element

linking devices, but they signal different kinds of thought relationships between parts of the sentence.

Finally, the writer should be cautioned to avoid using the dash as a catch-all mark of punctuation, one that indiscriminately substitutes for periods, commas, semicolons, etc.

44

Use a pair of dashes to enclose abrupt parenthetical elements that occur within a sentence.

—— ——

Examples:

1 ✔ In some instances— —although no one will admit it— —the police overreacted to the provocation.

2 ✔ What surprised everyone when the measure came to a vote was the chairperson's reluctance— —indeed, downright refusal— —to allow any riders to be attached to the bill.

3 ✔ One of them— —let me call him Jim Prude— —is clean-shaven and dresses like a successful businessman.

4 ✔ Their unhappiness is due to the ease with which envy is aroused and the difficulty— —or should I say impossibility? — —of fighting against it.

5 ✔ Yet despite the similarities in their travelogues— —for indeed the same trip inspired both works— —the two reports differ in some key aspects.

The three devices used to set off parenthetical elements in written prose are dashes, parentheses, and commas. The kind of parenthetical element that should be enclosed with a pair of dashes is the kind that interrupts the normal syntactical flow of the sentence. What characterizes such elements in the examples above is that they abruptly arrest the normal flow of the sentence to add some qualifying or rectifying information. The rhetorical effect of the enclosing dashes is to give the parenthetical element an unusual measure of emphasis.

A pair of parentheses is another typographical device used to mark off parenthetical elements in a sentence. Enclosure within parentheses is used mainly for those elements that merely add information or identification, as in sentences like these:

> All the companies that used the service were charged a small fee (usually $500) and were required to sign a contract (an "exclusive-use" agreement).

> The manager of each franchise is expected to report monthly to NARM (National Association of Retail Merchants) and to "rotate" (take turns doing various jobs) every two weeks.

The typographical device used to set off the mildest kind of interrupting element is a pair of commas. Whether to enclose a parenthetical element with commas or with parentheses or with dashes is more a matter of stylistic choice than a matter of grammatical necessity. There are degrees of interruption and emphasis, and with practice, a writer develops an instinct for knowing when to mark off parenthetical elements with commas (lowest degree of interruption and emphasis), when to mark them off with parentheses (middle degree), and when to mark them off with dashes (highest degree). Consider the degrees of interruption and emphasis in the following sentences:

Parents, as we have since learned, reported the incident directly to the school board.

During the postwar years (at least from 1946 to 1952), no one in the agency dared challenge a directive from higher up.

When the order was challenged, the clerk—some claim it was his wife—put a call through to the manager.

45

A dash is made on the typewriter with two unspaced hyphens and with no space before the dash or after the dash. (In handwriting, the dash should be made slightly longer than a hyphen.)

Example:

He forgot——if he ever knew——the functions of the

various marks of punctuation.

Do not hit the space bar on the typewriter *before* the first hyphen, *between* the first and second hyphen, or *after* the second hyphen. In short, do not hit the space bar at all in forming the dash on the typewriter.

Mechanics

Introduction

The graphic devices dealt with in this section might be, and often are, classified as punctuation. But because such graphic devices as italics, capitalization, and numbers are not correlated—as punctuation marks are—with the intonational patterns of the spoken language, these devices are grouped in a separate section under the heading Mechanics. In the spoken language, a word printed with a capital letter is pronounced no differently from the same word printed with a lower-case letter. Nor is the italicized title of a book pronounced any differently from that same title printed without italics. (Italics used for emphasizing a word or phrase, however, do correspond to stress in the spoken language.) Even quotation marks, which one might regard as correlated with the spoken language, do not correspond to anything the voice does when it quotes direct speech.

But whether one classifies these graphic devices as punctuation or as mechanics is immaterial. What is important to remember is that these devices are part of the written language exclusively and that they facilitate the reading of that language. Most readers would have at least momentary difficulty making sense of the following string of words:

barbara replied in canada people use gas to refer to the liquid propellant that is called petrol in most other english speaking countries.

If the proper punctuation and mechanics were used with that string of words, readers would be spared the momentary difficulty:

Barbara replied, "In Canada, people use *gas* to refer to the liquid propellant that is called *petrol* in most other English-speaking countries."

Deprived of the resources that the human voice has to clarify the meaning of a spoken utterance, writers should be eager to use all those typographical devices that make it easier for readers to grasp what they are trying to convey in the written medium.

46

The period or the comma always goes inside the closing quotation mark.

," ."

Examples:

1 ✔ The author announces at the beginning of his article that he is going to cite only "facts."

2 ✔ "I know," she said, "that you are telling me a barefaced lie."

3 ✔ Mrs. Robinson's "bearded, sandalled, unwashed hippies," many of whom had travelled over sixteen hundred kilometres to the festival, represented an aggregation of straight-A students.

Mechanics

This is a clear case where usage, rather than logic, has established the prevailing convention. Many reputable British printers put the period or comma *outside* the closing quotation mark, especially when the quotation marks enclose something less than a complete sentence—e.g., a word or phrase or dependent clause. But North American printers almost universally put the period or comma *inside* the closing quotation mark.

The advantage of such consistency is that you never have to pause and ask yourself, "Is this a case where the period goes inside or outside the quotation mark?" Whether it is a single word or a phrase or a dependent clause or an independent clause that is enclosed, the period or comma always goes *inside* the closing quotation mark.

In handwriting or in typewriting, take care to put the period or comma *inside* the quotation mark, not *under* it like this:', '. In the case of quotations within quotations, both the single-stroke quotation mark and the double-stroke quotation go *outside* the period or the comma, as in this example:

> "I read recently," he stated, "that Percy Faith said, 'Eighty cents of the recording dollar is spent by kids between the ages of nine and sixteen.' "

47

The colon or semicolon always goes outside the closing quotation mark.

48 Closing Quotation Mark, with Question Mark

Examples:

1 ✔He called this schedule of activities his "load**"**: work, study, exercise, recreation, and sleep.
2 ✔He told his taunters, "I refuse to budge**"**; his knees, however, were shaking even as he said those words.

Whereas the period or the comma always goes *inside* the closing quotation mark, the colon or the semicolon always goes *outside* it. If writers have occasion to use quotation marks with a colon or a semicolon, they have only to recall that the convention governing the relationship of the colon or the semicolon to the closing quotation mark is just the opposite of the convention for the period and the comma.

48

The question mark sometimes goes inside, sometimes outside, the closing quotation mark.

?"   **"?**

Examples:

1 ✔Who was it that said, "I regret that I have but one life to lose for my country**"?**
2 ✔He asked her bluntly, "Will you marry me**?"**
3 ✔When will they stop asking, "Who then is responsible for the war**?"**

Although a period or a comma always goes inside the closing quotation mark and a colon or a semicolon always goes outside it, you have to consider each case individually before

Mechanics

deciding whether to put the question mark inside or outside the closing quotation mark. Fortunately, the criteria for determining whether it goes inside or outside the quotation mark are fairly simple to apply:

(a) When the whole sentence, but not the unit enclosed in question marks, is a question, the question mark goes *outside* the closing quotation mark. (See example **1**.)

(b) When only the unit enclosed in quotation marks is a question, the question mark goes *inside* the closing quotation mark. (See example **2**.)

(c) When the whole sentence and the unit enclosed in quotation marks are both questions, the question mark goes *inside* the closing quotation mark. (See example **3**.)

In all cases, the question mark serves as the terminal punctuation for the entire sentence. In (*b*), you do not add a period outside the closing quotation mark, and in (*c*), you do not add another question mark outside the closing quotation mark.

49

The titles of books, newspapers, magazines, professional journals, plays, long poems, movies, radio programs, television programs, long musical compositions, works of art, and ships should be italicized in print or underlined in handwriting and typewriting.

Examples:

1 ✔Some of the themes that Atwood mentions in *Survival* can be found in her novel *The Edible Woman*.
(titles of books)

2 ✔He has already published three articles in the *Canadian Journal of Education*.
(title of a professional journal)

3 ✔ To support his contention, he quoted a passage from an anonymous article in *Maclean's*.
(title of a magazine)

4 ✔ The moonship *Falcon* settled down about 400 m from the projected landing site.
(title of the Apollo 15 "ship")

5 ✔ My parents insisted on watching *The Undersea World of Jacques Cousteau*.
(title of a television program)

6 ✔ The critics unanimously panned the recent performance of *La Traviata*.
(title of an opera)

Printers use a special italic type, which slants slightly to the right, to set off certain words in a sentence from other words that are printed in regular roman type (upright letters). When the main body of the text is set in italic type, the situation is reversed, and words to be set off are set in regular roman type. In handwriting or typewriting, one sets off words by underlining them. For example, sentence **1** when handwritten or typewritten would appear as follows:

> Some of the themes that Atwood mentions in <u>Survival</u> can be found in her novel <u>The Edible Woman</u>.

Although italics are used with the titles of all of the items listed above, the writer most often has occasion to use italics with the titles of book-length or pamphlet-length published materials. Besides being a convention, the use of italics for

Mechanics

titles can also protect meaning in some instances. If someone wrote "I didn't really like Huckleberry Finn," readers
might be uncertain (unless the context gave them a clue)
whether the writer was revealing dislike for Mark Twain's
noval or for the character of that name in the novel. If the
writer intended to indicate a dislike for the novel, that mes-
sage could be conveyed unambiguously by simply underlining (italicizing) the proper name.

How does one decide whether a poem is long enough to
have its title italicized? As with most relative matters, the
extreme cases are easily determinable. Obviously, a sonnet
would not qualify as a long poem, but Milton's *Paradise Lost*
would. It is the middle-length poem that causes indecision.
A reliable rule of thumb is this: if the poem was ever published as a separate book, or if it could conceivably be
published as a separate book, it could be considered long
enough to be set forth in italics. According to that guideline,
T.S. Eliot's *The Wasteland* would be considered a long poem,
but his "The Love Song of J. Alfred Prufrock" would be
considered a short poem and therefore should be enclosed
in quotation marks (see **50**). But if you cannot decide whether
a poem is "long" or "short," either italicize the title or enclose
it in quotation marks and use that system consistently
throughout the paper.

50

The titles of articles, essays, short stories, short poems, songs, and chapters of books should be enclosed in quotation marks.

Examples:

1 ✔ Thomas Gray's "Elegy Written in a Country Churchyard" is reputed to be the most anthologized poem in the English language.
(title of a short poem)

2 ✔ Hollis Alpert's "Movies Are Better Than the Stage" first appeared in the *Saturday Review of Literature.*
(title of an article in a periodical)

3 ✔ Alice Munro's "The Dance of the Happy Shades" was reprinted in 1968 in the second series of *Canadian Short Stories.*
(title of a short story in a collection of stories.)

4 ✔ The song "Raindrops Keep Falling on My Head" set exactly the right mood for the bicycle caper in the movie *Butch Cassidy and the Sundance Kid.*
(title of a song)

The general rule here is that the titles of published material that is *part* of a book or a periodical should be enclosed in quotation marks.

The title of a paper that you write should not be enclosed in quotation marks, nor should it be italicized. If your title contains elements that are normally italicized or enclosed in quotation marks, those elements, of course, should be italicized or enclosed in quotation marks.

Mechanics

The right and the wrong formats of a title for a paper submitted for a class assignment or for publication are illustrated here:

WRONG: **X** "The Evolution of Courtly Love in Medieval Literature"

<u>The Evolution of Courtly Love in Medieval Literature</u>

RIGHT ✔ The Evolution of Courtly Love in Medieval Literature

The Evolution of Courtly Love in Chaucer's <u>Troilus and Criseyde</u>

Courtly Love in Herrick's "Corinna's Going a-Maying" and Marvell's "To His Coy Mistress"

The Shift in Meaning of the Word <u>Love</u> in Renaissance Lyrics

"One Giant Step for Mankind"—Historic Words for an Historic Occasion

51

Italicize (underline) words referred to as words.

Examples of reference words as words:

1 ✔He questioned the appropriateness of *honesty* in this context.
2 ✔The *Dictionary of Canadian English* defines *drone* as "a male bee especially a male honey bee."
3 ✔Unquestionably, *trudged* is a more specific verb than *walked*.
4 ✔Look, for example, at his use of purely subjective words like *marvellous, exquisite,* and *wondrous.*

51 Underlined Words

"He questioned the appropriateness of honesty in this context."

"He questioned the appropriateness of *honesty* in this context."

Although composed of the same words in the same order, those two sentences carry different meanings. The first sentence signifies that what is being challenged is the appropriateness of the thing (the abstract quality) designated by the word *honesty;* the second sentence signifies that what is being questioned is the appropriateness of the word itself. It is the italics alone that indicate to the reader the difference in meaning between these two sentences.

Italics (underlining) are a graphic device commonly used to distinguish a word being used *as a word* from that same word used as a symbol for an idea. (In handwritten or typewritten copy, you italicize words by underlining them.) An alternative but less common device for marking words used as words is to enclose the words in quotation marks, as in this example:

> The heavy use of such sensory diction as "creaking hinges," "piercing scream," and "muffled thud" helps to evoke the scene and make it more exciting to the reader.

Since both devices are authorized by convention, the writer should adopt one system and use it consistently. The use of italics is probably the safer of the two systems, however, because quotation marks are also used to enclose quoted words and phrases, as in the sentence, We heard her say "yes." (Here *yes* is not being referred to as a word but is a quotation of what she said.)

Mechanics

52

**Italicize (underline) foreign words and phrases,
unless they have become naturalized or anglicized.**

Examples of foreign words and phrases:

1 ✔ The opposition stages a **coup d'état** in France.

2 ✔ We appointed an **ad hoc** committee to make several changes
in the curriculum.

3 ✔ There had been a remarkable revival in the late 1960s of the
Weltschmerz that characterized the poetry of the Romantics.

So that the reader will not be even momentarily mystified by
the sudden intrusion of strange-looking words into a stream
of English words, printers use italics to emphasize foreign
words and phrases. The graphic device of italics does not
ensure, of course, that the reader will be able to translate
the foreign locution, but it does prevent confusion by alerting
the reader to the presence of non-English words.

Some foreign words and phrases, like habeas corpus,
divorcee, mania, siesta, subpoena, have been used so often
in an English context that they have been accepted into the
vocabulary as "naturalized" English words and therefore as
not needing to be set forth in italics. Dictionaries have a
system for indicating which foreign words and phrases have
become naturalized and which have *not* become naturalized. Since dictionaries sometimes differ in their judgements
about the naturalized status of certain foreign expressions,
writers should consistently follow the dictates of the dictionary available to them in determining whether a word or
phrase needs italics.

53 Hyphen, for Compound Words

An obvious exception to the rule is that proper nouns designating foreign persons, places, and institutions, even when they retain their native spelling and pronunciation, are *always* set forth without italics (underlining).

53

Compound words should be hyphenated.

Examples of compound words:

1 ✔Because I had the normal six-year-old's "sweet tooth," I was irresistibly lured by the candy store.

2 ✔He was attracted to anti-Establishment movements because they lacked policy-making administrators

3 ✔They scheduled the examinations in three-quarter-hour segments.

4 ✔ He preferred eighteenth-century literature because of its urbanity.

5 ✔A five-or six-storey building should be all you will need for that kind of plant operation.

English reveals its Germanic origins in its tendency to form compounds—that is, to take two or more existent words and join them together to create a single unit that designates a thing or a concept quite different from what the individual words designate. A familiar example is the word **basketball.** When the two distinct words **basket** and **ball** were first joined to designate an athletic game or the kind of ball used in that

Mechanics

game, the words were linked by a hyphen: **basket-ball.**
When repeated use had made this new compound familiar
to readers, the hyphen was dropped, and the two words
were printed as a single word with no break between the
two constituent parts.

Dozens of words in English have made this transition from
a hyphenated compound to a single amalgamated word
(e.g., *mailman, skyscraper, airport*). But hundreds of compounds are still printed with a hyphen, either because they
have not been used enough to achieve status as unmarked
hybrids or because the absence of a hyphen would lead to
ambiguity. A reliable dictionary will indicate which compounds have made the passage and which have not.

With the exception of those words that have become recognized amalgams, a hyphen should be used to link

(a) two or more words functioning as a single grammatical unit.

his **never-say-die** attitude (adjective)
the junkyard had a huge **car-crusher** (noun)
the hoodlums **pistol-whipped** him (verb)
he conceded the point **willy-nilly** (adverb)

(b) two-word numbers (from 21 to 99) when they are
written out.

twenty-one, thirty-six, forty-eight, ninety-nine

(c) combinations with prefixes **ex-** and **self-.**
ex-chairman, ex-wife, self-denial, self-contradictory

(d) combinations with prefixes like **anti-, pro-, pre-,
post-,** when the second element of the combinations begins

53 Hyphen, for Compound Words

with a capital letter or a number.

anti-Establishment, pro-Canadian, pre-1929, post-1945

(e) combinations with prefixes **like anti-, pro-, pre-, re-, semi-, sub-, over-,** when the second element begins with the letter that occurs at the end of the prefix.

anti-intellectual, pro-oxidant, pre-election, re-entry, semi-independent, sub-basement, over-refined (with a few exceptions, like **overrun** and **override**).

(f) combinations where the unhyphenated compound might be mistaken for another word.

re-cover (the chair)	**resign** (his office)
recover (the lost wallet)	**co-op**
re-sign (the contract)	**coop**

With these exceptions, compounds formed with these prefixes now tend to be written as a single word (e.g., *antiknock, predetermined, postgraduate*). And at least one authority would have all the compounds in (*e*), above, spelled solid. As against this, other authorities make distinctions that allow for *preelection* and *reentry* while prohibiting *antiintellectual*. In adopting any system that makes such distinctions, the writer should consistently follow the conventions of the authority consulted.

Frequently in writing, only a hyphen will clarify ambiguous syntax. If the writer of sample sentence **3** had not used hyphens **(They scheduled the examinations in three quarter hour segments),** the reader would not be able to determine whether the examination was divided into three fifteen-minute segments (a meaning that would be clearly signalled by this placement of the hyphen: **three quarter-hour segments**) or whether it was divided into forty-five-

Mechanics

minute segments (a meaning that is clearly signalled by this placement of hyphens: **three-quarter-hour segments**). There is a similar ambiguity in the sentence "He was the only new car dealer in town." A speaker would be able to clarify the ambiguous syntax of that sentence by the appropriate intonation of the voice. But in writing, only a hyphen will make clear whether the writer meant to say "He was the only new **car-dealer** in town" or "He was the only **new-car** dealer in town."

Sample sentence **5** shows how to hyphenate when there is more than one term on the left side of the hyphenation **(five-, six-).** In this way **storey** need not be repeated (as in **A five-storey or six-storey building. . .**). In typing, a space   is inserted after the hyphen if it does not immediately precede the word it is meant to join **(five- or;** NOT: **five-or).**

54

A word can be broken and hyphenated at the end of a line only at a syllable break; a one-syllable word can never be broken and hyphenated.

Most dictionaries supply two valuable bits of information by the initial entry of every word: (1) the spelling of the word, and (2) the syllabification of the word. The word **belligerent,** for instance, is entered this way in the dictionary: **bel • lig • er • ent.** If that word occurred at the end of a line and you saw that you could not get the whole word in the remaining space, you could break the word and hyphenate it at any of the syllables marked with a raised period. But you could not break the word in any of the following places: **bell-igerent, belli-gerent, bellige-rent.**

Since the syllabification of English words is often unpredictable, it is safest to consult a dictionary when you are in doubt about where syllable breaks occur. But after a while, you learn certain "tricks" about syllabification that save you a trip to the dictionary. A word can usually be broken

(a) after a prefix **(con-, ad-, pre-, un-, im-).**
(b) before a suffix **(-tion, -ment, -less, -ous, -ing).**
(c) between double consonants **(oc-cur-rence, cop-per, prig-gish).**

One-syllable words, however, can never be divided and hyphenated, no matter how long they are. So if you come to the end of the line and find that you do not have enough space to squeeze in single-syllable words like *horde, grieve, stopped, quaint, strength, wrenched,* leave the space blank and write the whole word on the next line. You have no choice.

Even in the interest of preserving a right-hand margin, you should not divide a word so that only one or two letters of it stand at the end of the line or at the beginning of the next line. Faced with divisions like *a-bout, o-cean, un-healthy, grass-y, dioram-a, flo-rid, smok-er, live-ly,* you should put the whole word on that line or the next one. Remember that the hyphen itself takes up one space.

Mechanics

55

Observe the conventions governing the use of numbers in written copy.

Examples of violations of the conventions:

1 X 522 men reported to the emergency headquarters.

2 X During the first half of the **20th** century **95 3-**year high schools and **14 4-**year high schools adopted the semester system.

3 X The wedding reception started at **four P.M. in the afternoon.**

4 X An account of the Wall Street crash of October **twenty-ninth, nineteen hundred and twenty-nine** begins on page **fifty-five.**

5 X About **six and a half %** of the stores were selling a gross of index cards for more than **thirty-six dollars and thirty-eight cents.**

The most common conventions governing the use of numbers in written copy are as follows:

(a) Do not begin a sentence with an Arabic number; spell out the number or recast the sentence:

1 ✓ Five hundred and twenty-two men reported to the emergency headquarters.

OR: A total of **522** men reported to the emergency headquarters.

(b) Spell out any number of less than three digits (or any number under 101) when the number is used as an adjective modifying a noun:

2 ✓ During the first half of the **twentieth** century, **ninety-five three-**year high schools and **fourteen four-**year high schools adopted the semester system.

55 Numbers, in Written Copy

(c) Always use Arabic numbers with A.M. and P.M. and do not add the redundant **o'clock** and **morning** or **afternoon:**

3 ✔The wedding reception started at **4:00** P.M.
OR: The wedding reception started at **four o'clock in the afternoon.**

Note that according to *Canadian SI Metric* Practice the time of day may be designated by using either the word **o'clock** or the twenty-four-hour system. If you use the word **o'clock,** always spell out the number. The abbreviations A.M. and P.M. are never used in twenty-four-hour clock.

The wedding reception started at **four o'clock.**

If you use the twenty-four-hour system, always use Arabic numbers and do not add the redundant **h** (for hours) or the phrases **in the morning** or **in the afternoon.**

The wedding reception started at **16:00.**

(d) Use Arabic numbers for dates and page numbers:

4 ✔ An account of the Wall Street crash of October **29, 1929** begins on page **55.**

(e) Use Arabic numbers for addresses (618 N. 29th St.), dollars and cents ($4.68, $0.15 or 15¢), decimals (3.14, 0.475), degrees (18°C), measurements (3 cm × 5 cm, 3.75 km, 75 cm, 3.2 m tall or three metres tall*), percentages (6% or 6 percent). But always use **per cent** with fractional percentages.

5 ✔ About **6 1/2 per cent** of the stores were selling a gross of index cards for more than **$36.38.**

* (For SI Metric abbreviations, see p. 242)

Mechanics

To conform to *Canadian SI Metric* practice, note that decimals are always used instead of fractions (**6.5%** not 6½%) and that the symbol **%** is always used, never the word per cent.

56

Observe the conventions governing the capitalization of certain words.

Examples:

1 ✔ **P**rime **M**inister **J**ohn **D**iefenbaker informed the **M**embers of **P**arliament that he was not appointing **M**s. **S**heila **B**lack as the **C**anadian ambassador to the **U**nited **S**tates.
2 ✔ **T**he title of the article in the *New Yorker* was "**T**he **T**ime of **I**llusion."
3 ✔ **D**r. **C**. **H**ampson, a professor in the **F**aculty of **E**ducation at the **U**niversity of **A**lberta, has been observing the feeding habits of migratory birds captured in the **A**rctic and the **P**acific **N**orthwest.
4 ✔ The prime vacation time for most **C**anadians is the period between **C**anada **D**ay and **L**abour **D**ay.
5 ✔ **T**he **K**orean troops resisted the invasion of the **C**ommunist forces.

In general, the convention governing capitalization is that the first letter of the proper name (that is, the particular or exclusive name) of persons, places, things, institutions, agencies, etc., should be capitalized. While the tendency today is to use lower case letters for many words that formerly were written or printed with capital letters, the use of capital letters still prevails in the following cases:

56 Capitalization, of Certain Words

(a) The first letter of the first word of a sentence.

They were uncertain about which words should be capitalized.

(b) The first letter of the first word of every line of traditional English verse.

Little fly,
Thy summer's play
My thoughtless hand
Has brushed away.

(c) All nouns, pronouns, verbs, adjectives, adverbs, and first and last words of titles of publications and other artistic works.

Remembrance of Things Past (see **49**)
"The Place of the Enthymeme in Rhetorical Theory" (see **50**)
A Tent That Families Can Live In"
Gone with the Wind

(d) The first name, middle name or initial, and last name of a person, real or fictional.

J.A. Macdonald	Adele Mona Nyberg
David Copperfield	Achilles

(e) The names and abbreviations of villages, towns, cities, counties, provinces, nations, and regions.

Melville, Saskatchewan	County of Lacombe
U.S.A.	Soviet Union
Indo-China	Arctic Circle
the Western World	South America
the Midwestern states	the North (but: we drove south)

Mechanics

(f)   The names of rivers, lakes, falls, oceans, mountains, deserts, parks.

the **M**ississippi **R**iver
Rocky **M**ountains
Lake **E**rie

Atlantic
Jasper **N**ational **P**ark
Niagara **F**alls

(g)   The names and abbreviations of businesses, industries, institutions, agencies, schools, political parties, religious denominations, and philosophical, literary, and artistic movements.

University of **N**ew **B**runswick
the **L**iberal convention
Dow **C**hemical **C**orporation
Communist(s) (but: a communist ideology)
Victorian literature
Existential philosophy

Conservatives
N.D.P.
Wiley **P**ublishers of **C**anada Ltd.
Smithsonian **I**nstitution
Japan **A**ir **L**ines
the **H**ouse of **C**ommons
Pure **L**and **B**uddhism

(h)   The titles of historical events, epochs, and periods.

Renaissance
World **W**ar II
the **M**iddle **A**ges
Reformation

Thirty **Y**ears' **W**ar
Ice **A**ge
the **B**attle of **D**unkerque
the **D**epression

(i)   Honourary and official titles when they precede the name of the person and when they are used in place of the name of the specific person.

former **P**rime **M**inister **P**earson
the **D**uke of **C**ornwall
Pope **P**aul
His (**H**er) **E**xcellency

Governor-**G**eneral **M**assey
Lord **M**ountbatten
the **C**hief **J**ustice
Queen **E**lizabeth
Sri **R**amakrishna

56 Capitalization, of Certain Words

(j)   The names of weekdays, months, holidays, holy days, and other special days or periods.

Christmas Eve	Remembrance Day
Passover	Canada Day
Lent	National Book Week
Mardi Gras	the first Sunday in June

(k)   The names and abbreviations of the books and divisions of the Bible and other sacred books (no italics for these titles).

Genesis	Pentateuch
Matt. (Gospel of Matthew)	Acts of the Apostles
Epistle to the Romans	Vulgate
King James Version	Koran
Talmud	Scriptures
Book of Job	Bhagavad Gita
Pss. (Psalms)	Lotus Sutra

Exceptions: Do not capitalize words like the underlined in the following examples:

the African coast (but: the West Coast)	the river Elbe (but: the Elbe River)
northern Manitoba	the federal government
the politician from Nova Scotia	the county courthouse
	the municipal library

Format of the Research Paper

General Instructions

A research paper reports the results of some investigation, experiment, interview, or reading that you have done. Some of the ordinary papers you write are also based on personal investigations, interviews, and reading, and when they are based on external sources, you should acknowledge those sources in the text of your paper. For instance, you can reveal the source of information or quotations by saying in the text "Mr. Stanley Smith, the director of the Outward Bound project, with whom I talked last week, confirmed the rumour that..." or "James Reston said in his column in last Sunday's *New York Times* that...". Authors of research papers also use identifying lead-ins like those in the text, but in addition they supply, in footnotes, any further bibliographical information (for instance, the exact date of the newspaper they are quoting from and the number of the page on which the passage occurred) that readers would need if they wanted to check the sources. By revealing this specific information about the source, authors enhance their credibility and enable their readers to check whether the report is accurate or fair.

In the pages that follow, we will present some advice about gathering and reporting material from outside sources, some models for footnote and bibliographical forms, and a sample research paper. The instructor or the journal that you write for may prescribe a format that differs from the advice given here, but if no specific instructions are given, you can follow these suggestions and models with the assurance that they conform to the prevailing conventions for research papers.

(A) GATHERING NOTES

Each researcher eventually discovers his or her own system of gathering notes. Some people, for instance, just scribble their notes on full sheets of paper or in spiral notebooks. The system that works best for most researchers, however, is to record notes and quotations on 8 cm × 12 cm or 10 cm × 15 cm cards—*one* note or quotation to a card. The advantage of having your notes on cards is that later you can select and arrange the cards to suit the order in which you are going to use them in your paper. It is considerably more difficult to select and arrange notes if they are written out, one after the other, on full sheets of paper.

(B) SELF-CONTAINED NOTE CARDS

Each note card should be self-contained—that is, it should contain all the information you would need to document that material properly if you used it in your paper. A note card is self-contained if you never have to go back to the original source to recover any bit of information about the note. So each note card should carry at least this much information:

1 The card should carry some indication whether the note is paraphrased or quoted verbatim. Don't trust your memory to be able to distinguish later whether a note is paraphrased or quoted.

Format of the Research Paper

2 If quoted material covers more than one page in the source from which it was copied, you should devise some system of indicating just where the quoted material went over to the next page. If later you use only part of that quotation, you have to know whether to cite one page (p. 189) or two pages (pp. 189–90) in the footnote. Some notation like (→ p. 190) inserted in the note card after the last word on the page (in this case, after the last word on p. 189) in the original source will help you determine later whether you need to cite one page or two pages.

3 The note card should contain all the bibliographical information needed to document the note in a footnote of your paper: name of the author, title of the book or article, publication information, and page numbers (see Model Footnotes). If you are taking several notes from the same source, you can devise some shorthand system so that you do not have to write out all the bibliographical information on every note card.

(C) WHAT NEEDS TO BE FOOTNOTED?

You will have to develop a sense for what needs to be documented with a footnote. Here are some guidelines to help you:

1 Ordinarily, every direct quotation should carry a footnote. However, if you were doing a research paper on, say, a novel, you could be spared having to document every quotation from the novel by using a footnote like this the *first time* you quoted from the novel:

[8]Hugh MacLennan, The Watch That Ends the Night (Toronto: Macmillan, 1961), p. 73. Hereafter all quotations will be documented with a page number in parentheses immediately after the quotation.

2 Paraphrased material may or may not need a footnote. If the fact or information that you report in your own words is *generally known* by people knowledgeable on the subject, you probably would not have to document that paraphrased material. For instance, if you were writing a research paper on Confederation, you probably would not have to document your statement that the date of Confederation was July 1, 1867, because that historical fact is common knowledge. But if one of the sections in your paper dealt with the dates on which Manitoba and British Columbia joined Confederation, you would have to document July 15, 1870 and July 21, 1871. When, however, you cannot resolve your doubt about whether paraphrased material needs to be documented with a footnote that reveals the source of the information, document it.

3 When you are summarizing, in your own words, a great deal of information that you have gathered from your reading, you can be spared having to document several sentences in that summary by putting a footnote number after the *first sentence* of the summary and using a footnote like this:

> 10For the biographical information presented in this and the subsequent paragraph, I am indebted to Minnie M. Brashear, Mark Twain: Son of Missouri (Chapel Hill: University of North Carolina Press, 1934), pp. 34-65 and Gamaliel Bradford, "Mark Twain," Atlantic Monthly, 125 (April, 1920), 462-73.

(D) KEEP QUOTATIONS TO A MINIMUM

A research paper should not be just a pastiche of long quotations stitched together by an occasional comment or by a transitional sentence by the author of the paper. You

Format of the Research Paper

should use your own words as much as possible, and when you do quote, you should keep the quotation brief. Often a quoted phrase or sentence will make a point more emphatically than a long quotation. You must learn to look for the phrase or sentence that represents the kernel of the quotation and to use that extract rather than the full quotation. Otherwise, the point you want to make with the quotation may be lost in all the verbiage. You will be more likely to keep your quotations short if you try to work most of the quotations into the framework of your own sentence, like this:

Northrop Frye argues that improvement does not occur in the arts themselves, but in "the comprehension of them, and the refining of society which results from it. It is the consumer, not the producer, who benefits by culture, the consumer who becomes humanized and liberally educated."[12]

Sometimes, however, when you find it difficult to present the essential point in a short extract, you will have to quote something at greater length. Long quotations (two sentences or more) should be *inset* from the left-hand margin and *single-spaced,* with *no quotation marks enclosing the quotation,* like this:

> Marshall MacLuhan mentions how the development of
> the printing press affected political thought:
>
>> Print multiplied scholars, but it also diminished
>> their social and political importance. And it did
>> the same for books. Unexpectedly, print fostered
>> nationalism and broke down international
>> communication.[15]

(E) USE A LEAD-IN FOR ALL QUOTATIONS

Every direct quotation should be accompanied by a lead-in phrase or clause, which at least identifies by name the person who is about to speak. But it further aids coherence if the lead-in also points up the pertinence of the subsequent quotation to what you have been talking about or to what you are going to talk about. Here are some typical identifying and orienting lead-ins:

> Robert Weaver goes on to say that "Canadian short-
> story writers have often had to persevere in thin soil."
> "By the middle 1770s," says Arthur Lower in <u>Colony</u>
> <u>to Nation</u>, "English traders had got into territory
> never before touched by white men, well beyond the

Format of the Research Paper

limit of the La Verendrye journeys."[3]

MacLuhan continues with this explanation of Dickens' popular success:

Following this last lead-in would be either a single sentence enclosed in quotation marks or a series of sentences inset and single-spaced, like the extended quotation in (D) above.

(F)   THE FORMAT OF FOOTNOTES

The first line of every footnote is indented from the left-hand margin (usually the same number of spaces as paragraph indentations in the body of the paper), but any subsequent lines of the same footnote are brought out to the left-hand margin. If footnotes are put at the bottom of the page, they are single-spaced *within* the footnote and double-spaced *between* footnotes. If footnotes are put on separate pages they are single-spaced *within* the footnote and double-spaced *between* footnotes for classroom assignments. For publication, footnotes put on separate pages are double-spaced both within the footnote and between footnotes. See Model Footnotes and the Sample Research Paper for further information about the format of footnotes.

(G) PRIMARY AND SECONDARY FOOTNOTES

Primary footnote forms (that is, those giving full bibliographical information) must be used the *first time* a source is cited. Thereafter, that same source can be documented with a secondary footnote form (that is, a shortened form). See Model Footnotes and the Model Research Paper for the format of primary and secondary footnotes (pp. 147, 162).

(H) THE FORMAT OF BIBLIOGRAPHICAL ENTRIES

Bibliographical entries are arranged alphabetically on separate pages at the end of the research paper. The list of entries is alphabetized according to the last name of the author (or, in the case of unsigned articles, according to the first significant word in the title). For that reason, the names of authors are inverted in the bibliography—e.g., **Heilman, Robert.** The first line of each bibliographical entry begins at the left-hand margin, and any subsequent lines in that entry are indented (just the opposite of the format of footnotes). Bibliographical entries are single-spaced *within* the entry and double-spaced *between* entries. (If, however, the paper is being submitted for publication, the bibliographical entries are double-spaced both within the entry and between entries.) See Models for Bibliography (p. 155) for other differences between the format of footnotes and the format of bibliographical entries.

Format of the Research Paper

(I) ELLIPSIS PERIODS

Ellipsis periods (three spaced periods) are used to indicate that words or whole sentences have been omitted from a direct quotation:

> The Prime Minister said last week that "the Canadian people ... would not tolerate such violence."

Note that there is a space between periods. Periods used without spacing (...) would be wrong.

> Northrop Frye gives us this description of writing in early Canada:
>
>> The editorial writer attacking the Family Compact, the preacher demolishing imaginary atheists with the argument of design, are using words aggressively .... Ideas are weapons; one seeks the verbal coup de grace, the irrefutable refutation.

The fourth *period in this instance is the period used to mark the end of the sentence. Because of this period and the capital letter with which the next group of words begins, we know that at least the end of the first sentence has been omitted and that possibly as much as a whole paragraph has been removed before the next sentence.*

Usually there is no need to put ellipsis periods at the beginning or end of a quotation, because the reader knows that the quotation has been extracted from a larger context. Reserve ellipsis periods for indicating omissions *within* quotations.

(J)   SQUARE BRACKETS

Square brackets are used to enclose anything that the author of the research paper inserts into a direct quotation from another author:

> About this tendency to indulge in scatological language, H.A. Taine wrote, "He [Swift] drags poetry not only through the mud, but into the filth; he rolls in it like a raging madman, he enthrones himself in it, and bespatters all passers-by.
>
> The Member of Parliament was emphatic in stating his reaction to the measure: "This action by the AIB [Anti-Inflation Board] will definitely not reverse the upward spiral [of prices and wages] that has plagued us for the past several years."

Format of the Research Paper

We find this entry in the Japanese admiral's diary:
"Promptly at 8:32 on Sunday morning of December 6
[sic], 1941, I dispatched the first wave of bombers for
the raid on Perl Harber [sic]."

Sic *is a Latin adverb meaning "thus," "in this manner,"
and is used to let the reader know that the error in logic
or fact or grammar or spelling in the quotation has been
copied exactly as it was in the original source. It is italicized because it is a foreign word.*

If your typewriter does not have keys that make square
brackets, you will have to draw the brackets with a pen after
you remove the paper from the typewriter.

Model Footnotes

The models for footnotes and for bibliography follow the forms prescribed in *The MLA Style Sheet*, 2nd ed. (New York: Modern Language Association, 1970), and in the much fuller *MLA Handbook* (New York: Modern Language Association, 1977). The MLA system of documentation is the most widely used system in North America for scholarly manuscripts in the humanities.

The models here are single-spaced within the footnote and double-spaced between footnotes, as they would be if they appeared at the bottom of the page in a research paper or a dissertation. For the double-spacing of footnotes, see the Model for Footnotes Entered on Separate Pages on p. 166.

For the bibliography form for each of these model footnotes, see the next section (p. 157).

(K) PRIMARY FOOTNOTES
(the first reference to a source)

(1) A single book by a single author:

[14]John Mitchell, The Adolescent Predicament (Toronto: Holt, Rinehart & Winston of Canada Limited, 1975), p. 88.

Format of the Research Paper

> [8]Brian S. Powell, <u>Making Poetry</u> (Don Mills, Ont.:
> Collier-Macmillan Canada Ltd., 1973) pp. 78-9.

*Notice that the first line of the footnote is indented and that subsequent lines of the footnote start at the left-hand margin. The **p.** is the abbreviation of **page; pp.** is the abbreviation of **pages.***

(2) A single book by more than one author:

> [12]Thomas E. Curtis and Wilma W. Bidwell,
> <u>Curriculum and Instruction for Emerging Adolescents</u>
> (Don Mills, Ont.: Addison-Wesley (Canada) Ltd., 1977),
> p. 251.

(3) A book of more than one volume:

> [13]William Lee Hays and Robert L. Winkler,
> <u>Statistics: Probability, Inference, and Decision</u> (New
> York: Holt, Rinehart, & Winston, Inc., 1970), II, 137.

*Whenever a volume number is cited (here the Roman numeral **II**), the abbreviation **p.** or **pp.** is not used in front of the page number.*

(4) A book edited by one or more editors:

> [3]<u>Reflections</u>, ed. James B. Bell and Earl W. Buxton
> (Toronto: Wiley Publishers of Canada Limited, 1975),
> pp. 83-4.

⁹The Letters of Jonathan Swift to Charles Ford, ed. David Nichol Smith (Oxford: Clarendon Press, 1935), p. 187.

*Here the abbreviation **ed.** stands for **edited by.***

(5) An essay or a chapter by an author in an edited collection:

²Martin J. Svaglic, "Classical Rhetoric and Victorian Prose," The Art of Victorian Prose, ed. George Levine and William Madden (New York: Oxford University Press, 1968), pp. 268-70.

(6) A new edition of a book:

⁵Oswald Doughty, A Victorian Romantic, Dante Gabriel Rossetti, 2nd ed. (London: Oxford University Press, 1960), p. 35.

*Here the abbreviation **ed.** stands for **edition.***

(7) A book that is part of a series:

²⁶William Heytesbury, Medieval Logic and the Rise of Mathematical Physics. University of Wisconsin Publications in Medieval Science, No. 3 (Madison: University of Wisconsin Press, 1956) p. 97.

*Here the abbreviation **No.** stands for **Number.***

Format of the Research Paper

(8) A book in a paperback series:

> [11]Edmund Wilson, To the Finland Station. Anchor Books (Garden City, N.Y.: Doubleday, 1955), p. 130.

(9) A translation:

> [6]Fyodor Dostoevsky, Crime and Punishment, trans. Constance Garnett (New York: Heritage Press, 1938), p. 351.
>
> [7]Jacques Ellul, A Critique of the New Commonplaces, trans. Helen Weaver (New York: Knopf, 1968), pp. 139-40.

*The abbreviation **trans.** stands for **translated by.***

(10) A signed and an unsigned article from an encyclopedia:

> [4]J. A. Ewing, "Steam-Engines and Other Heat-Engines," Encyclopedia Britannica, 9th ed. XXII, 475-7.
>
> [10]"Dwarfed Trees," Encyclopedia Americana, 1948, XI, 445.

Since encyclopedias periodically undergo revision and updating, the particular edition consulted should be indicated by a date or a number. In the bibliography, unsigned articles are filed alphabetically according to the first significant word in the title—here Dwarfed.

Model Footnotes

(11) An article from a journal:

> [12]Nelson Adkins, "Emerson and the Bardic Tradition," <u>PMLA</u>, 72 (1948), 665.
>
> [8]Theodore Otto Windt, Jr., "The Diatribe: Last Resort for Protest," <u>QJS</u>, 58 (1972), 9-10.

Well-known scholarly journals are commonly referred to by their abbreviated titles. Here PMLA *stands for* Publications of the Modern Language Association; QJS *stands for* Quarterly Journal of Speech. *Volume numbers of journals are now designated by an Arabic number (here 72 and 58) rather than, as formerly, by a Roman numeral. Because the volume number has been cited, the abbreviations* p. *and* pp. *are not used in front of the page numbers.*

(12) An article in a popular magazine:

> [4]Robert Lewis, "Winning by Default," <u>Maclean's</u>, 21 February 1977, p. 26.
>
> [7]Charles E. Silberman, "Technology Is Knocking on the Schoolhouse Door," <u>Fortune</u>, Aug. 1966, pp. 121-2.

Note that Maclean's *is published once a week;* Fortune *is published once each month. Because no volume number is cited,* p. *and* pp. *are used in front of the page numbers.*

Format of the Research Paper

(13) A signed and an unsigned article in a newspaper:

> [15] Marvin Lipton, "Current Events," <u>Edmonton Journal</u>, 15 March 1977, p. 15.
>
> [26] "Twin Games Bid: Wrestling, Judo," <u>New York Times</u>, 9 April 1972, Section 5, p. 15, cols. 4-6.

For editions of a newspaper with multiple sections, each with its own pagination, it is necessary to cite the section in addition to the page number. It is helpful also to give column numbers. Sometimes, if an article appeared in one edition of a newspaper but not in other editions, it is necessary to specify the particular edition of the newspaper—e.g., New York Times, Late City Ed., 4 Feb. 1972, p. 12, col. 1.

(14) A signed book review:

> [19] John F. Dalbor, rev. of <u>Meaning and Mind: A Study in the Psychology of Language</u>, by Robert F. Terwilliger, <u>Philosophy & Rhetoric</u>, 5 (1972), 60-1.
>
> [3] Brendan Gill, rev. of <u>Ibsen</u>, by Michael Meyer, <u>New Yorker</u>, 8 April 1972, p. 128.

The first review appeared in a scholarly journal; the second review appeared in a weekly magazine. The abbreviation **rev.** *stands for* **review.**

(L) SECONDARY FOOTNOTES

(shortened forms after a source has once been given in full).

> [15]Mitchell, p. 88.

This is the shortened form of the first footnote given in (1) under Primary Footnotes.

> [16]Hays and Winkler, II, 137.

This is the shortened form of the footnote given in (3) under Primary Footnotes.

> [17]Ibid., I, 87.

***Ibid.** is the abbreviation of the Latin adverb **ibidem,** meaning "in the same place." Ibid. may be used if the source in that footnote is the same as the one cited in the immediately preceding footnote. However, if a reader would have to turn back one or more pages to find the last source cited, it would be better to use the last-name shortened form: Hays and Winkler, I, 87. There must be added to Ibid. only what changes from the previous source. Thus in footnote 17 above, I and 87 were added to Ibid., because both the volume number and the page number changed from the previous footnote. If only the page number changed, footnote 17 would read thus: Ibid., p. 145. If nothing changed, footnote 17 would read thus: Ibid.*

Format of the Research Paper

[18]Wilson, <u>Finland Station,</u> pp. 220-2.

When more than one book or article by the same author has been cited in a paper, you must use an abbreviated title in addition to the surname of the author in order to identify the source. In footnote 18 above, Finland Station *is an abbreviated form of the full title* To the Finland Station.

[19]"Rendezvous with Ecology," p. 97.

In the case of an anonymous article or book, the title or a shortened form of it has to be used in subsequent references to that source.

Models for Bibliography

The form of a bibliography entry differs in some ways from that of a footnote reference. The following shows how the two forms handle a citation for the same book.

BIBLIOGRAPHY FORM

Frye, Northrop. <u>Anatomy of Criticism</u>. Princeton, N.J.: Princeton University Press, 1957.

FOOTNOTE FORM

[8]Northrop Frye, <u>Anatomy of Criticism</u> (Princeton, N.J.: Princeton University Press, 1957), p. 225.

BIBLIOGRAPHY	FOOTNOTE
(a) The first line begins at the left-hand margin, with all subsequent lines indented.	(a) The first line is indented, with all subsequent lines brought out to the left-hand margin.

155

Format of the Research Paper

(b) The name of the author is inverted (last name first) for purposes of alphabetizing the list of entries.

(b) The name of the author is set down in the normal order.

(c) The three main divisions of author, title, and publishing data are separated by periods.

(c) The three main divisions of author, title, and publishing data are separated by commas.

(d) Place of publication, name of the publisher, and publication date follow the title, without parentheses.

(d) Place of publication, name of the publisher, and publication date are enclosed in parentheses.

(e) The subtitle, if any, should be included in the citation. See (3) below.

(e) The subtitle, if any, may be omitted in the citation.

(f) There is no page reference unless the entry is for an article or part of a collection, in which case the full span of pages (first page and last page) is cited.

(f) Only a specified page reference is cited.

Models for Bibliography

CORRESPONDING BIBLIOGRAPHY FORMS FOR THE
FOURTEEN MODEL FOOTNOTES

If the research paper is being submitted to a journal for possible publication, the entries should be double-spaced both within the entry and between the entries. If, however, the paper is submitted as an assignment in a course, the bibliography entries may be single-spaced within the entry and double-spaced between entries, as they are in these models.

(1) A single book by a single author:

Mitchell, John. The Adolescent Predicament. Toronto: Holt, Rinehart & Winston of Canada Limited, 1975.

Powell, Brian S. Making Poetry. Don Mills, Ont.: Collier-Macmillan Canada Ltd., 1973.

(2) A single book by more than one author:

Curtis, Thomas E., and Wilma W. Bidwell. Curriculum and Instruction for Emerging Adolescents. Don Mills, Ont.: Addison-Wesley (Canada) Ltd., 1971.

Only the name of the first author should be inverted.

(3) A book of more than one volume:

Hays, William Lee, and Robert L. Winkler. Statistics: Probability, Inference, and Decision. 2 vols. New York: Holt, Rinehart & Winston Inc., 1970.

Format of the Research Paper

(4) A book edited by one or more editors:

The Letters of Jonathan Swift to Charles Ford. Ed.
David Nichol Smith. Oxford: Clarendon Press,
1935.

Reflections. Ed. James B. Bell and Earl W. Buxton.
Toronto: Wiley Publishers of Canada Limited,
1975.

*In the bibliography, these books would be filed alpha-
betically according to the first significant word in the title—
Letters and **Reflections** respectively.*

(5) An essay or a chapter by an author in an edited collection:

Svaglic, Martin J. "Classical Rhetoric and Victorian
Prose." The Art of Victorian Prose. Ed. George
Levine and William Madden. New York: Oxford
University Press, 1968, pp. 268-88.

*Because this essay is part of a collection, the full span
of pages is cited in the bibliography.*

(6) A new edition of a book:

Doughty, Oswald. A Victorian Romantic, Dante Gabriel
Rossetti. 2nd ed. London: Oxford University Press,
1960.

(7) A book that is part of a series:

> Heytesbury, William. <u>Medieval Logic and the Rise of Mathematical Physics</u>. University of Wisconsin Publications in Medieval Science, No. 3. Madison: University of Wisconsin Press, 1956.

(8) A book in a paperback series:

> Wilson, Edmund. <u>To the Finland Station</u>. Anchor Books. Garden City, N.Y.: Doubleday, 1955.

(9) A translation:

> Dostoevsky, Fyodor. <u>Crime and Punishment</u>. Trans. Constance Garnett. New York: Heritage Press, 1938.

> Ellul, Jacques. <u>A Critique of the New Commonplaces</u>. Trans. Helen Weaver. New York: Knopf, 1968.

(10) A signed and an unsigned article from an encyclopedia:

> Ewing, J.A. "Steam-Engines and Other Heat-Engines." <u>Encyclopedia Britannica</u>. 9th ed., XXII, 473-526.

> "Dwarfed Trees." <u>Encyclopedia Americana</u>. 1948, IX, 445-6.

Notice that the full span of pages of these articles is given.

Format of the Research Paper

(11) An article from a journal:

Adkins, Nelson. "Emerson and the Bardic Tradition."
Publications of the Modern Language Association,
72 (1948), 662-7.

Windt, Theodore Otto, Jr. "The Diatribe: Last Resort
for Protest." Quarterly Journal of Speech, 58
(1972), 1-14.

*Although in footnotes well-known scholarly journals are
commonly referred to by their abbreviated title, it is advisable to give the full title in the bibliography.*

(12) An article in a popular magazine:

Lewis, Robert. "Winning by Default." Maclean's, 21
February 1977, pp. 26-9.

Silberman, Charles E. "Technology Is Knocking on the
Schoolhouse Door." Fortune, Aug. 1966, pp. 120-
25.

(13) A signed and an unsigned article in a newspaper:

Lipton, Marvin. "Current Events." Edmonton Journal,
15 March 1977, p. 15.

"Twin Games Bid: Wrestling, Judo." New York Times,
9 April 1972, Section 5, p. 15, cols. 4-6.

(14) A signed book review:

Dalbor, John B. Review of <u>Meaning and Mind: A Study in the Psychology of Language</u>, by Robert F. Terwilliger. <u>Philosophy & Rhetoric</u>, 5 (1972), 60-61.

Gill, Brendan. Review of <u>Ibsen</u>, by Michael Meyer. <u>New Yorker</u>, 8 April 1972, pp. 126-30.

Format of the Research Paper

Model Research Paper (with footnotes at bottom of page) and Bibliography

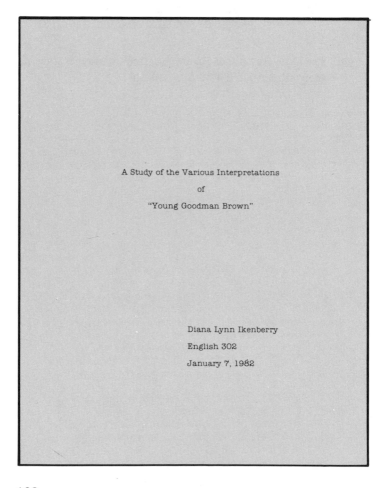

A Study of the Various Interpretations

of

"Young Goodman Brown"

Diana Lynn Ikenberry

English 302

January 7, 1982

A Study of the Various Interpretations

of

"Young Goodman Brown"

Nathaniel Hawthorne's "Young Goodman Brown"
has been the subject of many different interpretations.
The story is such an ambiguous one that critics have
seldom been able to agree on the meaning of a number
of its parts. Among the questions that have engaged
many critics is that of whether Goodman Brown
actually went into the forest and met the devil or
whether he only dreamed that he did. Richard Fogle is
one critic who believes that Hawthorne failed to
answer this question definitively because "the
ambiguities of meaning are intentional, an integral
part of his purpose."[1] Fogle feels that the ambiguity
results from unanswered questions like the one above,
and it is just this ambiguity or "device of multiple
choice,"[2] as Fogle calls it, that is the very essence of
"Young Goodman Brown."

Critic Thomas F. Walsh, Jr., has gone a step
further in analyzing the ambiguity of Brown's journey
into the forest.[3] Although, like Fogle, he feels that the

---

[1] Richard H. Fogle, "Ambiguity and Clarity in
Hawthorne's 'Young Goodman Brown,' " New England
Quarterly, 18 (December 1945), 448.

[2] Ibid., p. 449.

[3] Thomas F. Walsh, Jr., "The Bedeviling of Young
Goodman Brown," Modern Language Quarterly, 19
(December 1958), 331-6.

Format of the Research Paper

reader can never be certain whether the journey was real or imaginary, he points out that the reader can be certain "not only of the nature and stages of Goodman Brown's despair, but also of its probable cause."[4] The effect upon Brown, once he emerges from the forest, is also quite clear: "Goodman Brown lived and died an unhappy, despairing man."[5] According to Walsh, the key to interpreting the ambiguous forest sequence lies in the story's complex symbolic pattern.

D.M. McKeithan's view of Brown's journey is unlike any of the previously mentioned views. He contends that Goodman Brown neither journeyed into the forest that night nor dreamed that he did. What Brown did do, according to McKeithan, was "to indulge in sin (represented by the journey into the forest that night . . .)" thinking that he could break away from his sinfulness whenever he chose to,[6] However, Brown indulged in sin longer than he expected and "suffered the consequences, which were the loss of religious faith and faith in all other human beings."[7]

All of these interpretations shed some light on the nature of Hawthorne's story, and they will form the basis of our discussion. More clues as to Hawthorne's intentions may be found in the comments of

---

[4]Ibid., p. 332.

[5]Walsh, p. 336.

[6]D.M. McKeithan, "Hawthorne's 'Young Goodman Brown': An Interpretation," Modern Language Notes, 67 (February 1952), 96.

[7]Ibid.

BIBLIOGRAPHY

Connolly, Thomas E. "Hawthorne's 'Young Goodman
    Brown': An Attack on Puritanic Calvinism,"
    American Literature, 28 (November 1956),
    370-5.

Fogle, Richard H. "Ambiguity and Clarity in
    Hawthorne's 'Young Goodman Brown'" New
    England Quarterly, 18 (December 1945),
    448-465.

Hawthorne, Nathaniel. "Young Goodman Brown,"
    Nathaniel Hawthorne: Young Goodman Brown,
    ed. Thomas E. Connolly. Columbus, Ohio: Charles
    E. Merrill Publishing Company, 1968, pp. 10-21.

McKeithan, D.M. "Hawthorne's 'Young Goodman
    Brown': An Interpretation." Modern Language
    Notes, 67 (February 1952), 93-6.

Matthews, James W. "Antinomianism in 'Young
    Goodman Brown,'" Studies in Short Fiction, 3
    (Fall 1965), 73-5.

Miller, Paul W. "Hawthorne's 'Young Goodman
    Brown': Cynicism or Meliorism? "Nineteenth-
    Century Fiction, 14 (December 1959), 255-264.

Schneider, Herbert W. The Puritan Mind. New York:
    Henry Holt and Company, 1930.

Walsh, Thomas F., Jr. "The Bedeviling of Young
    Goodman Brown," Modern Language Quarterly,
    19 (December 1958), 331-6.

*The bibliography for a paper submitted as a classroom as-
signment may be single-spaced within entries, as it is in the
model above. The bibliography for a paper submitted for
publication, however, should be double-spaced, both within
the entry and between entries. Notice that the entries above
are arranged in alphabetical order.*

Format of the Research Paper

Model for Footnotes Entered on Separate Pages

If a paper is submitted for publication, the footnotes must be entered on separate pages and must be double-spaced both within and between footnotes. If, however, footnotes are entered on separate pages at the end of a research paper submitted as a **classroom assignment,** they should be **single-spaced** within the footnote and double-spaced between the footnotes, as they are in the model below.

[1]All my quotations from the "Elegy" are taken from the final approved version of 1753, as printed in Herbert W. Starr and John R. Hendrickson, eds., The Complete Poems of Thomas Gray, English, Latin, and Greek (Oxford: Clarendon Press, 1966). Hereafter, quotations from this edition of the poem will be documented by line numbers in parentheses.

[2]Samuel Johnson, "Gray," The Lives of the English Poets, ed. George Birkbeck Hill (Oxford: Clarendon Press, 1905), III, 442.

[3]Odell Shephard, "A Youth to Fortune and to Fame Unknown," Modern Philology, 20 (1923), 347-73.

[4]Ibid., p. 348.

[5]A detailed description of the various manuscript versions is given in Francis G. Stokes, ed., <u>An Elegy Written in a Country Churchyard</u> (Oxford: Clarendon Press, 1929), pp. 23-6. Herbert W. Starr has also presented an illuminating study of the successive versions of the poem in his article "Gray's Craftsmanship," <u>JEGP</u>, 45 (1946), 415-29.

[6]Shephard, p. 366.

[7]Ibid., pp. 371-2.

[8]H.W. Starr, "'A Youth to Fortune and to Fame Unknown': A Re-estimation," <u>JEGP</u>, 48 (1949), 97-107.

The APA System of Documentation

If the MLA system of documentation, illustrated in the previous section, is predominant in the humanities, the American Psychological Association (APA) system is predominant in such fields as psychology, education, psycholinguistics, and many of the social sciences. The highlights of this system will be presented here; for a fuller treatment, consult the readily available paperback edition of *Publication Manual of the American Psychological Association*, 2nd ed. (Washington, D.C.: American Psychological Association, 1974).

The two principal differences between the MLA and the APA systems are as follows:

(1) Whereas the MLA system documents quotations and other kinds of references in footnotes printed either at the

Format of the Research Paper

bottom of the page or on separate pages, the APA system documents all citations *within parentheses in the text.*

(2) Whereas the MLA system supplies complete bibliographic information about a work the first time that work is cited in a footnote, the APA system supplies only the *last name of the author, the publication date of the work,* and sometimes the *page number.*

Here is how the first reference to a book would be documented, first in the MLA style and then in the APA style:

MLA STYLE

[3]Mina P. Shaughnessy, <u>Errors and Expectations: A Guide for the Teacher of Basic Writing</u> (New York: Oxford University Press, 1977), p. 57.

APA STYLE

(Shaughnessy, 1977, p. 57).

Readers who wanted fuller information about the work cited in the parenthetical reference could turn to the list of references on a separate page, at the end of the paper. There, in an alphabetical listing, the Shaughnessy work would be entered in double-spaced typescript as follows:

Shaughnessy, M.P. <u>Errors and expectations: A guide for the teacher of basic writing</u>. New York: Oxford University Press, 1977.

The APA System of Documentation

VARIATIONS ON THE BASIC APA STYLE
OF DOCUMENTATION

(a) If a whole work is being referred to, only the author's last name and the date of the work are given in parentheses.

> A recent study has confirmed that twelve-year-olds
>
> grow at an amazingly rapid rate (Swanson, 1969).

(b) A page number or a chapter number is supplied only if part of a work is being referred to. Quotations always demand the addition of a page number.

> The committee boldly declared that "morality could
>
> not be enforced, but it could be bought" (Dawson,
>
> 1975, p. 105).

(c) Any information supplied in the text itself need not be repeated in the parentheses.

> Anderson (1948) found that only middle-class
>
> Europeans disdained our cultural values.
>
> In 1965, Miller professed his fervent admiration of
>
> our admissions policy.

(d) If a work has two authors, both authors should be cited each time a reference is made to that text. If a work

Format of the Research Paper

has three or more authors, all the authors should be cited the first time, but subsequently only the name of the first author followed by **et al.** needs to be given.

> The circulation of false rumours poisoned the environment of that conference (Getty & Howard, 1979).
>
> The overall effect of the smear tactics was a marked decline in voter interest (Abraham, Davis & Keppler, 1952).
>
> In three successive national elections, voters from Slavic neighborhoods showed a 72% turnout (Abraham et al., 1952, pp. 324-327).

(e) If several works are cited at the same point in the text, the works should be arranged alphabetically according to the last name of the author and should be separated with semicolons.

> All the studies of the problem agree that the proposed remedy is worse than the malady (Brown & Turkell, 1964; Firkins, 1960; Howells, 1949; Jackson, Miller, & Naylor, undated; Kameron, in press).

The APA System of Documentation

(f)   If several works by the same author are cited in the same reference, the works are distinguished by the publication dates, arranged in chronological order and separated with commas. Two or more works published by the same author in the same year are distinguished by the letters **a, b, c,** etc., added to the repeated date. In such chronological listings, works "in press" are always listed last.

> A consistent view on this point has been repeatedly
>
> expressed by the Canadian member of the Commission
>
> (Holden, 1959, 1965, 1970, 1971a, 1971b, 1976).

(g)   If no author is given for a work, two or three words from another part of the entry (usually from the title) should be used to refer to the work.

> The voters' apathy was decried in the final spring
>
> meeting of the city council ("The Gradual Decline,"
>
> 1976).

LIST OF REFERENCES

The *References* page appended to a paper that observes the APA style is comparable to, and yet different from, the *Bibliography* page in a paper that observes the MLA style. Both systems give full bibliographic information about the works cited in the body of the writing, and both systems arrange the entries alphabetically according to the last name of the author. In both systems, the names of the authors are inverted (surname first), but in the APA system, only the

Format of the Research Paper

initials of first and middle names are given, and when there are two or more authors for a work, the names of *all* the authors are inverted.

The conventions of sequence, punctuation, and capitalization in the APA style for the *References* section can most easily be illustrated with examples.

(1) A book by a single author:

> Luria, A. R. The working brain: An introduction to neuro-psychology. London: Penguin, 1973.

Note that the title of the book is underlined but that only the first word of the title and the first word following the colon in the title are capitalized. (Any proper nouns in a title would also be capitalized; see the following example.) The three main parts of an entry—author, title, and publication data—are separated with periods.

(2) A book by several authors:

> Koslin, S., Koslin, B.L., Pargament, R., & Pendelton, S. An evaluation of fifth grade reading programs in ten Toronto area school boards. 1973-1974. Toronto: Transmetro Research Institute, 1975.

Note that the names of all the authors are inverted, that the names are separated with commas, and that an ampersand (**&**) is put before the last name in the series, even when there are only two names, as in the following example:

The APA System of Documentation

(3) An article in an edited collection:

> Bobrow, D. G., and Norman, D. A. Some principles of memory schemata. In D. G. Bobrow & A. M. Collins (Eds.), Representation and understanding: Studies in cognitive science. New York: Academic Press, 1975.

Note that the title of the article (**Some principles,** etc.) is not enclosed in quotation marks and that only the first word of this title is capitalized. (Any proper nouns in the title of the article would, of course, be capitalized.) Note also that the subsequent names of the two editors (**Eds.**) of the collection are not inverted and that there is no comma between the names.

(4) An article in a journal:

> Stahl, A. The structure of children's compositions: Developmental and ethnic differences. Research in the Teaching of English, 1977, 11, 156-163.

Note that all substantive words in the title of the journal are capitalized and that the title of the journal is underlined. Note also that the year comes before the volume number and that the volume number (*11*) is underlined. For a journal that begins the numbering of its pages with page 1 in each issue, the number of the issue should be indicated with an Arabic number following the volume number—*11(3)*.

Format of the Research Paper

(5) A book by a corporate author:

American Psychological Association. <u>Standards for
educational and psychological tests and manuals</u>.
Washington, DC: Author, 1966.

Books and articles with corporate authors are listed alphabetically according to the first significant word of the entry (in this case, **American**). The word **Author** listed with the publication data indicates that the publisher of the work is the same as the group named in the author slot. If, however, the publisher is different from the corporate author, the name of that publisher would be given right after the place of publication.

These five models cover most of the kinds of published material likely to be used in a research paper. For additional models, consult the *Publication Manual of the American Psychological Association* (2nd ed.).

For an illustration of the physical appearance, in typescript, of a research paper and of a *References* page done according to the APA system of documentation, see the following pages, taken from a twenty-one-page article by Carl Bereiter of the Ontario Institute for Studies in Education: "Development in Writing," in *Testing, Teaching and Learning* (Washington, D.C.: National Institute of Education, 1979), pp. 146-166. This article was later reprinted in its entirety in L. W. Gregg and E. R. Steinberg, eds., *Cognitive Processes in Writing* (Hillsdale, N.J.: Erlbaum, 1979).

DEVELOPMENT IN WRITING

Carl Bereiter

Although there is a substantial body of data on the development of writing skills, it has not seemed to have much implication for instruction. Reviews of writing research from an educational perspective have given scant attention to it (Blount, 1973; Braddock, Lloyd-Jones, & Schoer, 1963; Lyman, 1929; West, 1967). Generally speaking, developmental research has educational significance only when there is a conceptual apparatus linking it with questions of practical significance.

Almost all of the data on writing development consist of frequency counts--words per communication unit, incidence of different kinds of dependent clauses, frequency of different types of writing at different ages, and so on. The conceptual frameworks used for interpreting these data have come largely from linguistics (e.g., Hunt, 1965; Loban, 1976; O'Donnell, Griffin, & Norris, 1967). However informative these analyses might be to the student of language development, they are disappointing from an educational point of view. The variables they look at seem unrelated to commonly held purposes of writing instruction (Nystrand, 1977).

The purpose of this paper is to synthesize findings on the growth of writing skills within what may be called an "applied cognitive-developmental"

Format of the Research Paper

framework. Key issues within an applied cognitive-developmental framework are the cognitive strategies children use and how these are adapted to their limited information processing capacities (Case, 1975, 1978; Klahr & Wallace, 1976; Scardamalia, in press). Although this paper will not deal with instructional implications, it will become evident that the issues considered within an applied cognitive-developmental framework are relevant to such concerns of writing instruction as fluency, coherence, correctness, sense of audience, style, and thought content.

What Is Development in Writing?

Students' writing will undoubtedly reflect their overall language development (Loban, 1976; O'Donnell et al., 1967) and also their level of cognitive development (Collis & Biggs, undated; Scardamalia, in press). It is to be expected that it will also at times reflect their level of moral development, social cognition, etc. Given the small role that writing plays in most children's lives, it is therefore reasonable to suppose that there is no such thing as writing development as such--that it is merely the resultant of other, more basic kinds of development. This view is implicit in the speech-primacy position of researchers like Loban (1963, 1966, 1976), who treat children's writing simply as another source of data on their language development.

APA-Style Research Paper

While it may be reasonable to treat writing development as a reflection of other kinds of development, it is not very useful to do so. An educationally relevant account of writing development would have to give prominence to whatever is distinctive about writing and potentially susceptible to direct influence. The following have been recognized as distinctive characteristics of writing.

1. Written English may be recognized as a subsystem of English, along with spoken English, and distinguishable from the latter in a number of ways. It is usually more compact, contains more elaborately specified subjects, and shows less local variation than spoken English, and generally shows a different distribution of linguistic devices and usages (Allen, 1972; Gleason, 1965; Long, 1961).

2. Written English and spoken English are predominately, but not

Format of the Research Paper

References

Allen, R.L. English grammars and English grammar. New York: Scribner's, 1972.

Blount, N.S. Research on teaching literature, language, and composition. In R. M. W. Travers (Ed.), Second handbook of research on teaching. Chicago: Rand-McNally, 1973.

Braddock, R., Lloyd-Jones, R., & Schoer, L. Research in written composition. Champaign, IL: National Council of Teachers of English, 1963.

Case, R. Gearing the demands of instruction to the developmental capacities of the learner. Review of Educational Research. 1975, 45(1), 59-87.

Case, R. Implications of developmental psychology for the design of effective instruction. In A. M. Lesgold, J. W. Pellegrino, S. D. Fokemma, & R. Glaser (Eds.), Cognitive psychology and instruction. Plenum, NY: Division of Plenum Publishing Corporation, 1978.

Collis, K. F., & Biggs, J. B. Classroom examples of cognitive development phenomena. ERDC Funded Project 7/41, University of Newcastle, undated.

Gleason, H. A., Jr. Linguistics and English grammar. New York: Holt, Rinehart & Winston, 1965.

Hunt, K. W. Grammatical structures written at three grade levels. Champaign, IL: National Council of Teachers of English, 1965. (Research Report No. 3.)

Klahr, D., & Wallace, J.G. Cognitive development: An information-processing view. Hillsdale, NJ: Erlbaum, 1976.

APA-Style Research Paper

Loban, W. Language development: Kindergarten through grade twelve. Urbana, IL: National Council of Teachers of English, 1976. (Research Report No. 18.)

Loban, W. The language of elementary school children. Urbana, IL: National Council of Teachers of English, 1963. (Research Report No. 1.)

Loban, W. Problems in oral English. Urbana, IL: National Council of Teachers of English, 1966. (Research Report No. 5.)

Long, R. B. The sentence and its parts: A grammar of contemporary English. Chicago: University of Chicago Press, 1961.

Lyman, R. Summary of investigation relating to grammar, language, and composition. Chicago: University of Chicago, 1929. (Supplementary educational Monographs, No. 36, published in conjunction with The School Review and The Elementary School Journal.)

Nystrand, M. Assessing written communication competence: A textual cognition model. Toronto, Canada: The Ontario Institute for Studies in Education, 1977. (ERIC Document Reproduction Service No. ED 133 732.)

O'Donnell, R. C., Griffin, W. J., & Norris, R. C. Syntax of kindergarten and elementary school children: A transformational analysis. Champaign, IL: National Council of Teachers of English, 1967. (Research Report No. 8.)

Scardamalia, M. How children cope with the cognitive demands of writing. In C. H. Frederiksen, M. S. Whiteman, & J. F. Dominic (Eds.), Writing: The nature, development, and teaching of written communication, in press.

West, W. W. Written composition. Review of Educational Research, 1967, 37(2), 159-167.

Formats for Letters

General Instructions

The one type of writing that most people engage in after they leave school is letter-writing. They will almost certainly write letters to parents, friends, and acquaintances; occasionally they may feel compelled to write a letter to the editor of a newspaper or magazine; and sometimes they may write more formal letters to institutions or officials for such purposes as applying for a job or requesting information or service. Although they do not have to be much concerned about the niceties of form when they are writing to intimate friends, they would be well advised to observe the conventions of form and etiquette in letters to people who are not close friends.

(A) FORMAT OF THE PERSONAL OR FAMILIAR LETTER

Letters written to acquaintances are commonly referred to as "personal letters." Although "anything goes" in letters to acquaintances, one should keep in mind that even the most intimate acquaintance is flattered if the author of the letter observes certain amenities of form. A model for a personal letter appears on p. 186. Here is a list of the conventions for the personal letter:

General Instructions

(a) Personal letters may be written on lined or unlined paper of any size, but usually they are written on note-size stationery.

(b) Personal letters may be handwritten and may occupy both sides of the page.

(c) Parts of the Personal Letter. The personal letter consists of **heading** (the sender's address), **date, salutation, body, complimentary closing,** and **signature.** It does not include the inside address (address of the person receiving the letter), which is always used in a business letter.

The Heading (the sender's address) is written at the top of the letter, beginning either halfway across the page or at the left margin.

The Date is written directly beneath the heading.

The Salutation is written several lines below the date, beginning at the left margin. It is usually followed by a comma, rather than by a colon. But if it is typed it is followed either by a colon or nothing. Depending on the degree of intimacy with the person receiving the letter, the sender can use salutations like these: **Dear Mom, Dear Jim, Dear Julie, Dear Ms. Worth.**

The Body may be written in indented paragraphs, single- or double-spaced.

The Complimentary Closing is written a few lines below the body (or typed a double-space below), beginning either halfway across the page or at the left margin (depending on where the heading began). Depending on the degree of intimacy with the person receiving the letter, the sender may use complimentary closings like these: **Much love, Affectionately, As ever, Cordially, Fondly, Sincerely.**

The Signature may include the sender's full name, or only a first name or nickname.

Formats for Letters

(B) FORMAT OF THE BUSINESS LETTER

Formal letters addressed to individuals in organizations are commonly called "business letters." The form of business letters is more strictly prescribed than that of personal letters. Models for a business letter appear on pp. 187 to 191. Here is a list of the conventions for the business letter:

(a) Business letters are written on 21 cm × 28 cm unlined paper or on 21 cm × 28 cm paper with a printed letterhead.

(b) Business letters must be typewritten, single-spaced, on one side of the page only.

(c) Parts of the Business Letter. The business letter consists of **letterhead, date, inside address, salutation, body, complimentary closing, signature,** and **reference initials.** These are the essential parts of the business letter. One or more of the following parts may also be included: **attention line** and/or **subject line** before the main body of the letter and **enclosure notation** and/or **carbon copy notation** after the reference initials.

Business letters may be typed in one of three styles: **full-block, semi-block,** or **semi-block with paragraph indentations,** and the letter parts are placed in different positions in each of these styles.

In full-block style, all letter parts (and first lines of paragraphs) begin at the left margin. In semi-block style, all letter parts (and first lines of paragraphs) begin at the left margin except the date, the complimentary closing, and the signature and company name, all of which begin half-way across the page. Semi-block style with paragraph indentations is just like semi-block except that the first line of paragraphs are also indented.

General Instructions

The Letterhead is usually printed at the top of the page. If it is not printed, it is typed, single-spaced, at the top of the page. In full-block style each line of the heading begins at the left margin. In semi-block style with or without paragraph indentations, each line begins halfway across the page.

The Date is typed on the line immediately below the heading. If the letter is typed on company letterhead, the date is typed on the second or third line below the letterhead. In full-block style the date begins at the left margin. In semi-block and indented styles it begins halfway across the page.

The Inside Address is the address of the person or organization receiving the letter and is typed in the same form on the envelope. It is typed single-spaced, usually five lines below the date. In all three styles each line of the inside address begins at the left margin.

The Salutation is typed two lines below the inside address, followed by a colon (if mixed or closed punctuation is used). In all three styles, it begins at the left margin. If the writer is addressing an organization rather than a specific person in that organization, salutations like **Gentlemen** or **Ladies** may be used. If the writer knows the name of the person, **Mr., Ms., Mrs. or Miss** should be used, followed by the last name: **Dear Mr. Nelson, Dear Miss Kupterberg, Dear Mrs. Graham, Dear Ms. Bendo.** Women who feel that marital status should be no more specified in their own case than in that of a man (for whom **Mr.** serves, irrespective of whether he is married) prefer **Ms.** to **Mrs.** or **Miss. Messrs.** is the plural of Mr.; **Mmes.** is the plural of **Mrs.; Misses** is the plural of **Miss.** Professional titles may also be used in the salutation: **Dear Professor Farmer, Dear Dr. Marton.** *(Webster's New Collegiate Dictionary* carries a list of the

Formats for Letters

forms of address to various dignitaries [judges, members of the clergy, bishops, et al.].)

The Body of the letter begins two lines below the salutation. It should be single-spaced except for double-spacing between paragraphs. In full-block and semi-block styles, paragraphs begin at the left margin. In indented style paragraphs are indented.

The Complimentary Closing is typed two lines below the body and followed by a comma (if mixed or closed punctuation is used). In full-block style it begins at the left margin. In semi-block and indented style, it begins halfway across the page. The usual complimentary closings for business letters are these: **Yours truly, Yours sincerely, Very truly yours, Sincerely, Sincerely yours.**

The Signature of the sender is typed four or five spaces below the complimentary closing (or below the company name if it has been included). In full-block style the signature begins at the left margin. In semi-block and indented styles, it begins halfway across the page. On the line below the typed name, however, the sender's official capacity may be typed (e.g., **President, Director of Personnel, Managing Editor**). The sender's name is signed in the space left between the complimentary closing and the typed signature.

The Reference Initials identify both the sender and the typist. They are typed two lines below the last line of the typed signature. In all three letter styles, they are typed at the left margin.

The following letter parts are often, but not always, included before the body of the business letter:

The Attention Line is used when the sender addresses the letter to an entire company but wants to direct the letter to one person within that company (e.g., **ATTENTION: Ms. Mary Pasquale**). It is typed two lines below the inside address and two lines above the salutation. In all letter styles, the attention line may begin at the left margin.

The Subject Line is used to emphasize the purpose of the letter (e.g., **SUBJECT: Policy no. 632**). It is typed two lines below the salutation and two lines above the main body of the letter. In all letter styles it may begin at the left margin. In semi-block style with paragraph indentations it may also be centred.

The following letter parts are sometimes included immediately after the reference initials:

The Enclosure Notation is used so that the receiver of the letter can tell just by glancing at the letter that something has been enclosed in the envelope. In all three letter styles, the enclosure notation consists of the word **Enclosure** or the abbreviation **Encl.**, typed on the line below the reference initials at the left margin.

The Carbon Copy Notation shows that a copy of the letter has been sent to someone else. In all three letter styles, the carbon copy notation consists of **cc** or **cc:** It is typed at the left margin on the line below the reference initials or enclosure notation, whichever comes last.

    cc: Mary Hunter
        Robert Allison

The following pages contain a model of a personal letter, outlines of the three styles of business letters, and a model business letter showing all business letter parts.

Formats for Letters

Sample Handwritten Personal Letter

11728 39A Ave.
Edmonton, AB
T6J 0P2

March 16, 1982

Dear Christine,

I'm going back to school tomorrow, and since I didn't get a chance to call you, I thought I'd just write a note.

Did Mom tell you about the Solar Energy project we're doing in science class? The solar collectors we built are in operation on the roof, helping to heat the lab's water. We'll be calculating the energy savings to the school board, and I'll write and tell you the results. Alberta winters are cold, but we think it'll work!

Love,
Julie

P.S. Say hi to Arthur!

Business Letter Styles: Full-Block

101 Underwood Avenue
Kentville, Nova Scotia
B4N 2G9
19 ___ 12 05

Fidelity Stereophonics Ltd.
1697 South Park Street
Halifax, Nova Scotia
B3J 2L4

Gentlemen:

Please send me _____

_____

_____

Yours truly,

Charlotte A. McIntyre

Charlotte A. McIntyre

Formats for Letters

Business Letter Styles: Semi-Block

101 Underwood Avenue
Kentville, Nova Scotia
B4N 2G9
19 ___ 12 05

Fidelity Stereophonics Ltd.
1697 South Park Street
Halifax, Nova Scotia
B3J 2L4

Gentlemen:

Please send me _____

_____

_____

Yours truly,

Charlotte A. McIntyre

Charlotte A. McIntyre

Business Letter Styles: Semi-Block
with Paragraph Indentations

101 Underwood Avenue
Kentville, Nova Scotia
B4N 2G9
19 ___ 12 05

Fidelity Stereophonics Ltd.
1697 South Park Street
Halifax, Nova Scotia
B3J 2L4

Gentlemen:

Please send me _____

_____

_____

Yours truly,

Charlotte A. McIntyre

Charlotte A. McIntyre

Formats for Letters

Models for Letter and Punctuation Styles

FULL-BLOCK

OPEN, OR NO-POINT,
PUNCTUATION

SEMI-BLOCK

MIXED, OR
TWO-POINT,
PUNCTUATION

SEMI-BLOCK

WITH PARAGRAPH INDENTATIONS

CLOSED, OR ALL-POINT,
PUNCTUATION

Churchill Life insurance co.

191 PORTAGE AVENUE, WINNIPEG, MANITOBA R3B 1Z7

May 18, 1982   date

Lemojuste Translation Services   inside address
58 Osborne Street N.
Winnipeg, Manitoba
R3C 1V1

ATTENTION: Mr. Robert Lapierre   attention line

Dear Mr. Lapierre: salutation

SUBJECT: Policy no. 607801   subject line

We have reviewed your translation of the above-mentioned   body
insurance policy and are quite pleased with your work,
which we found to be accurate and meticulous. One or two
minor changes were requested by our claims department
manager, and they are indicated on the enclosed copy of
the policy. If you could return your translation of these
changes within the next few days it would be greatly
appreciated.

Since our business in Quebec is expanding, we are planning
to have more of our policies translated in the near future.
We will certainly be in touch with you when more work is
available.

Thank you for your prompt completion of the job.

Yours truly,   complimentary closing

Theresa Kowalski   signature

Mrs. Theresa Kowalski
Underwriter

TK/dw   reference initials

Encl.   enclosure notation

cc: Jordan Simpson, Mary Valpone   carbon copy notation

Formats for Letters

Models for Addressing
Envelopes (reduced size)

PERSONAL LETTER

Julie Macchiusi
11728 39A Ave.
Edmonton, AB
T6J 0P8

Mrs. Christine Lawson
391 Riverside Dr.
Winnipeg, MB
R3M 1V6

BUSINESS LETTER ENVELOPE: PLAIN

Ms. Valerie Janek
211-19 Street North
Brandon, Manitoba
R7A 2V4

Churchill Life Insurance Company
191 Portage Avenue
Winnipeg, Manitoba
R3B 1Z7

Models for Addressing Envelopes

BUSINESS LETTER ENVELOPE: PREPRINTED

Mrs. Theresa Kowalski

Churchill Life insurance co.

191 PORTAGE AVENUE, WINNIPEG, MANITOBA R3B 1Z7

> Lemojuste Translation Services
> 58 Osborne Street N.
> Winnipeg, Manitoba
> R3C 1V1

ATTENTION: Mr. Robert Lapierre

Formats for Letters

Postal abbreviations for Canada and the United States

CANADIAN PROVINCES AND TERRITORIES

Alberta	AB	Nova Scotia	NS
British Columbia	BC	Ontario	ON
Manitoba	MB	Prince Edward Island	PE
New Brunswick	NB	Quebec	PQ
Newfoundland	NF	Saskatchewan	SK
Northwest Territories	NT	Yukon Territory	YT

UNITED STATES AND OUTLYING AREAS

Alabama	AL	Montana	MT
Alaska	AK	Nebraska	NB
Arizona	AZ	Nevada	NV
Arkansas	AR	New Hampshire	NH
California	CA	New Jersey	NJ
Colorado	CO	New Mexico	NM
Connecticut	CT	New York	NY
Delaware	DE	North Carolina	NC
District of Columbia	DC	North Dakota	ND
Florida	FL	Ohio	OH
Georgia	GA	Oklahoma	OK
Guam	GU	Oregon	OR
Hawaii	HI	Pennsylvania	PA
Idaho	ID	Puerto Rico	PR
Illinois	IL	Rhode Island	RI
Indiana	IN	South Carolina	SC
Iowa	IA	South Dakota	SD
Kansas	KS	Tennessee	TN
Kentucky	KY	Texas	TX
Louisiana	LA	Utah	UT
Maine	ME	Vermont	VT
Maryland	MD	Virgin Islands	VI
Massachusetts	MA	Virginia	VA
Michigan	MI	Washington	WA
Minnesota	MN	West Virginia	WV
Mississippi	MS	Wisconsin	WI
Missouri	MO	Wyoming	WY

A Résumé

A résumé (pronounced *réz-oo-may)* is a one- or two-page summary, presented in the form of a list, of a job-applicant's life, relevant personal experiences, education, work experience, extracurricular activities, awards, goals, etc. It is usually submitted, along with such documents as academic transcripts, letters of reference, and specimens of one's writing, as part of a formal application for a job. The résumé is also referred to using, and sometimes even labelled with, the Latin phrases *curriculum vitae* (the course of one's life) or *vita brevis* (a short life).

Under the headings of Education, Work Experience, and Extracurricular Activities, items are usually listed in a reverse chronological order, starting with the most recent and ending with the earliest. (See the sample résumé.)

Depending upon the kind of job being applied for, some of the other categories that could be included in a résumé are Travel, Languages, Community Service, Research, Publications, Teaching Experience.

A Résumé

RESUME

MARY WATSON EVANS

ADDRESS: 239 E. Torrence Rd.   BIRTHDATE: September 5, 1952
              Edmonton, Alberta
              T6J 1M4

TELEPHONE: (403) 448-1080
             (403) 474-2026

EDUCATION:

1975-77, M.Ed., University of Alberta, Edmonton, AB Major--Secondary English
1970-74, B.Ed., University of Calgary, Calgary, AB, graduated with honours, 1974
      Major--Secondary English
      Minor--French
1967-70, Ross Sheppard Composite High School, Edmonton, AB graduated
      with honours, 1970

WORK EXPERIENCE:

Graduate Teaching Assistant for Dr. James B. Bell, Professor of Education,
      University of Alberta, 1976-77
          Junior and Senior High School English teacher, Spruce Grove, AB, 1974-76
          Clerk-Typist, summer of 1972 and 1973, A-1 Tire Service, Edmonton, AB
          Swimming Instructor, summer of 1970 and 1971, Edmonton Parks and
            Recreation Dept., Edmonton, AB

EXTRACURRICULAR ACTIVITIES:

Secretary, Education Undergraduate Society, University of Calgary, 1971
Editor, Ross Sheppard newspaper, 1969
Secretary, Ross Sheppard Students' Union, 1970

AWARDS:

Tuition and fees, University of Calgary Undergraduate Bursary, 1973-74
$100 Province of Alberta Undergraduate Scholarship, 1971-72, 1972-73, 1973-74

CAREER GOALS:

English department head of senior high school

REFERENCES:

Mr. John Anderson   Dr. Robert James
Superintendent of Schools   Department of Secondary Education
County of Parkland Regional Office   The University of Alberta
Stony Plain, AB   Edmonton, AB
TOE 2G0   T6G 2G2

The Tenses of the English Verb

The following paradigms provide models for the tenses of regular verbs, irregular verbs, and the verb **to be** in Canadian English Usage or in what this text calls "public prose."

Regular verbs are those that usually form the past tense by adding **-ed** to the present tense of the verb (e.g., **walk — walked**). A few regular verbs, however, simply add **-d** (e.g., **hope — hoped**) or **-t** (e.g., **deal — dealt**) to form the past tense; and some regular verbs double the final consonant (e.g., **hop — hopped**) or change the final **y** to **i** (e.g., **copy — copied**) before adding **-ed.**

Irregular verbs are those that form the past tense by some change of spelling *within* the verb (e.g., **run — ran; drink — drank; weave — wove**).

A good desk dictionary will indicate which of the regular verbs form the past tense in ways other than simply adding **-ed** and will give the present, the past, and often the past-participle forms of irregular verbs (e.g., **eat, ate, eaten**). Here is the beginning of a typical dictionary entry that lists, in order, the present tense, the past tense, the past participle, and the present participle of an irregular verb. If you are in doubt about any of the forms of an irregular verb, consult your dictionary.

The Tenses of the English Verb

drive (drīv) v. *drove* or (Archaic) *drave, driv•en, driv•ing,* n.—v. **1** make go: Drive the dog away. Drive the nails into the board. Grief drove her insane. **2** force (into or out of some place, condition, act, etc.): Hunger drove him to steal. **3** direct the movement of (an automobile, a horsedrawn vehicle, etc.). **4** go or carry in an automobile, carriage, etc. **5** carry out with vigor; bring about: drive a bargain. **6** work hard or compel to work hard. **7** dash or rush with force: The ship drove on the rocks. **8** set in motion; supply power for: The wind drives the windmill.

With permission. From *Dictionary of Canadian English, The Senior Dictionary.* Copyright © 1967 by W. J. Gage Limited.

The Verb To Be

PRESENT TENSE	PAST TENSE	FUTURE TENSE
I **am** (cold)	I **was** (cold)	I **shall be** (cold)*
you **are**	you **were**	you **will be**
he/she/it **is**	he/she/it **was**	he/she/it **will be**
we are (cold)	we **were** (cold)	we **shall be** (cold)*
you **are**	you **were**	you **will be**
they **are**	they **were**	they **will be**

PERFECT TENSE	PAST PERFECT TENSE	FUTURE PERFECT TENSE
I **have been** (cold)	I **had been** (cold)	I **shall have been** (cold)*
you **have been**	you **had been**	you **will have been**
he/she/it **has been**	he/she/it **had been**	he/she/it **will have been**
we **have been** (cold)	we **had been** (cold)	we **shall have been** (cold)*
you **have been**	you **had been**	you **will have been**
they **have been**	they **had been**	they **will have been**

*Current usage also sanctions the use of **will** as the future-tense marker in the first person singular and plural.

ACTIVE VOICE
(The subject is the doer of the action.)

REGULAR VERBS	IRREGULAR VERBS

PRESENT TENSE

I **select** (the winner)	I **drive** (the car)
you **select**	you **drive**
he/she/it **selects**	he/she/it **drives**
we select (the winner)	we **drive** (the car)
you **select**	you **drive**
they **select**	they **drive**

PAST TENSE

I **selected** (the winner)	I **drove** (the car)
you **selected**	you **drove**
he/she/it **selected**	he/she/it **drove**
we **selected** (the winner)	we **drove** (the car)
you **selected**	you **drove**
they **selected**	they **drove**

FUTURE TENSE

I **shall select** (the winner)*	I **shall drive** (the car)*
you **will select**	you **will drive**
he/she/it **will select**	he/she/it **will drive**
we **shall select** (the winner)*	we **shall drive** (the car)*
you **will select**	you **will drive**
they **will select**	they **will drive**

The Tenses of the English Verb

PERFECT TENSE
I **have selected**
  (the winner)
you **have selected**
he/she/it **has selected**

we **have selected**
  (the winner)
you **have selected**
they **have selected**

PAST PERFECT TENSE
I **had selected** (the winner)
you **had selected**
he/she/it **had selected**

we **had selected** (the
  winner)
you **had selected**
they **had selected**

FUTURE PERFECT TENSE
I **shall have selected** (the
  winner)*
you **will have selected**
he/she/it **will have se-
lected**

we shall have selected (the
  winner)*
you **will have selected**
they **will have selected**

**PRESENT PERFECT
  TENSE**
I **have driven** (the car)
you **have driven**
he/she/it **has driven**

we **have driven** (the car)
you **have driven**
they **have driven**

PAST PERFECT TENSE
I **had driven** (the car)
you **had driven**
he/she/it **had driven**

we **had driven** (the car)
you **had driven**
they **had driven**

FUTURE PERFECT TENSE
I **shall have driven**
  (the car)*
you **will have driven**
he/she/it **will have driven**

we **shall have driven** (the
  car)*
you **will have driven**
they **will have driven**

PASSIVE VOICE
(The subject is the receiver of the action.)

The passive voice is often used when the writer wants to put the emphasis on the receiver of the action. In the sentence **The judges select me.**, the verb **select** is in the active voice. When the active voice is used, the doer of the action (**judges**) is the subject and goes before the verb. The receiver of the action (**me**) is the direct object and goes after the verb. Because the subject comes first, the reader pays more attention to it. How could this sentence be changed if the writer wanted to draw more attention to the object **me**? All the writer has to do is turn the object **me** into the subject **I** and change the verb into the passive voice (**am selected**). The previous subject, **judges,** can be left out altogether. The sentence will now read:

I am selected.

The subject **judges** can be left out altogether or they can be included at the end of the sentence:

I am selected by the judges.

Of course, since you can only change a verb into the passive voice by turning its direct object (**me**) into a subject **I**, any verb that does not have a direct object in the first place can never be changed into the passive voice. These verbs are called intransitive verbs. Verbs like **talk** are intransitive and don't take direct objects.

The Tenses of the English Verb

The following list shows all the tenses of two verbs in the passive voice. Notice that even though the past participle of the verb appears in *every* case (selected, driven), you only look at the form of the verb **to be** to find out the tense (**am** (selected) — **present; was** (selected) — **past, have been** (selected) — **present,** etc.)

REGULAR VERBS

PRESENT TENSE
I **am selected**
   (as the winner)
you **are selected**
he/she/it **is selected**

we **are selected** (as
   the winner)
you **are selected**
they **are selected**

PAST TENSE
I **was selected** (as the
   winner)
you **were selected**
he/she/it **was selected**

we **were selected** (as the
   winner)
you **were selected**
they **were selected**

IRREGULAR VERBS

PRESENT TENSE
I **am driven** (to school)
you **are driven**
he/she/it **is driven**

we **are driven** (to school)
you **are driven**
they **are driven**

PAST TENSE
I **was driven** (to school)
you **were driven**
he/she/it **was driven**

we **were driven** (to school)
you **were driven**
they **were driven**

FUTURE TENSE

I **shall be selected** (as the winner)*

you **will be selected**

he/she/it **will be selected**

we **shall be selected** (as the winner)*

you **will be selected**

they **will be selected**

PRESENT PERFECT TENSE

I **have been selected** (as the winner)

you **have been selected**

he/she/it **has been selected**

we **have been selected** (as the winner)

you **have been selected**

they **have been selected**

PAST PERFECT TENSE

I **had been selected** (as the winner)

you **had been selected**

he/she/it **had been selected**

we **had been selected** (as the winner)

you **had been selected**

they **had been selected**

FUTURE TENSE

I **shall be driven** (to school)*

you **will be driven**

he/she/it **will be driven**

we **shall be driven** (to school)*

you **will be driven**

they **will be driven**

PRESENT PERFECT TENSE

I **have been driven** (to school)

you **have been driven**

he/she/it **has been driven**

we **have been driven** (to school)

you **have been driven**

they **have been driven**

PAST PERFECT TENSE

I **had been driven** (to school)

you **had been driven**

he/she/it **had been driven**

we **had been driven** (to school)

you **had been driven**

they **had been driven**

The Tenses of the English Verb

FUTURE PERFECT TENSE

I **shall have been selected** (as the winner)*

you **will have been selected**

he/she/it **will have been selected**

we **shall have been selected** (as the winner)*

you **will have been selected**

they **will have been selected**

FUTURE PERFECT TENSE

I **shall have been driven** (to school)*

you **will have been driven**

he/she/it **will have been driven**

we **shall have been driven** (to school)*

you **will have been driven**

they **will have been driven**

Glossary of Usage

Many of the entries here deal with pairs of words that writers often confuse because the words look alike or sound alike. Ascertain the distinctions between these confusing pairs and then invent your own memorizing devices to help you make the right choice in a particular case. In all cases of disputed usage, the most conservative position on that usage is presented so that you can decide whether you can afford to run the risk of alienating that segment of your readers who subscribe to the conservative position.

affect, effect. The noun form is almost always **effect** (*The effect of the program was easily measured*). The wrong choices are usually made when writers use the verb. The verb **effect** means "to bring about," "to accomplish" (*The prisoner effected his escape by picking a lock*). The verb **affect** means "to influence" (*The weather affected the mood of the crowd.*)

allusion, illusion. Think of **allusion** as meaning "indirect reference" (*He made an allusion to her parents*). Think of **illusion** as meaning "a deceptive impression" (*The heat waves created the illusion of a lake in the desert*).

alot, a lot. This locution should always be written as two words (*A lot of the natives lost faith in the government.*)

The Little English Handbook

alright, allright, all right.   **All right** is the only correct way to write this expression (*He told his mother that he was all right*).

altogether, all together.   **Altogether** is the adverb form in the sense of "completely" (*She was not altogether happy with the present*). **All together** is the adjective form in the sense of "collectively" (*The students were all together in their loyalty to the team*).

among.   See **between**.

amount of, number of.   When you are speaking of masses or bulks, use **amount of** (*They bought a large amount of sugar*). When you are speaking of persons or things that can be counted one by one, use **number of** (*They bought a large number of cookies*). See **fewer, less**.

as, like.   See **like**

because of.   See **due to**

beside, besides.   Both of these words are used as prepositions, but **beside** means "at the side of" (*They built a cabin beside a lake*), and **besides** means "in addition to" (*Besides a pair of boots, they bought a jacket).*

between.   The conservative position is that between should be used only when two persons or things are involved (*They made a choice between the Democrat and the Republican*).

centre around.   One frequently sees and hears this expression (e.g. *His interest centred around his work*). The expression seems to violate the basic metaphor from which it derives. How can something centre **around** something else? Say instead *"His interest centred on his work"* or *"His interest centred upon his work."*

continual, continuous. There is a real distinction between these two adjectives. Think of **continual** as referring to something that occurs repeatedly (i.e. with interruptions). For instance, a noise that occurred every three or four minutes would be a "continual noise"; a noise that persisted without interruption for an hour would be a "continuous noise." **Continual** is stop-and-go; **continuous** is an uninterrupted flow.

could of, should of, would of. In the spoken language, these forms sound very much like the correct written forms. In writing, use the correct forms **could have, should have, would have** or, in informal contexts, the contractions **could've, should've, would've.**

data. The word **data**, like the words **criteria** and **phenomena**, is a plural noun and therefore demands the plural form of the demonstrative adjective (*these data, those data*) and the plural form of the verb (*These data present convincing evidence of his guilt. The data were submitted by the committee*).

different from, different than. In Canadian English usage, **different than** is the more commonly used phrase. It may be followed by a noun (*His musical experience is different than mine*) or by a noun clause (*His treatment is different than what we expected*).

disinterested, uninterested. Careful writers still make a distinction between these two words. For them, **disinterested** means "unbiased," "impartial," "objective" (*The mother could not make a disinterested judgment about her son*). **Uninterested**, for them, means "bored," "indifferent to" (*The students were obviously uninterested in the lecture*).

The Little English Handbook

due to, because of. Many writers use **due to** and **because of** interchangeably. Some writers, however, observe the conservative distinction between these two expressions: **due to** is an adjectival construction, and **because of** is an adverbial construction. Accordingly, these writers would always follow any form of the verb **to be** (**is, were, has been,** etc.) with **due to** (*Due to illness, he was absent all week*), and they would always follow transitive and intransitive verbs with the adverbial construction **because of** (*She missed the party because of illness. He failed because of illness*). Sometimes, they substitute **owing to** or **on account of** for **because of.**

effect. See **affect.**

fewer, less. Use **fewer** with countable items (*Louise has fewer hats than Emily does*). Use **less** when speaking of mass or bulk (*Elmer has less sand in his garden than Andrew does*). See **amount of, number of.**

good. This word is often used colloquially as an adverb (*The catcher played good*). Formal English, however, would use the adverb **well** to modify the verb played (*The catcher played well*).

imply, infer. There is a definite difference in meaning between these two verbs. **Imply** means "to hint at," "to suggest" (*She implied that she wouldn't come to his party*). **Infer** means "to deduce," "to draw a conclusion from" (*He inferred from the look on her face that she wouldn't come to his party*).

irregardless. This word is considered to be a double negative and should never be used. Use **regardless** instead.

kind of, sort of. Do not use the article **a** or **an** with either of these phrases (*He suffered some kind of a heart attack.*

She got the sort of an ovation she deserved). **Kind of** and **sort of** in the sense of "rather" or "somewhat" (*He was kind of annoyed with his teacher*) should be reserved for an informal or a colloquial context.

lend, loan. The conservative position is that **loan** should be used exclusively as a noun (*He took out a loan from the bank*) and that **lend** should be used exclusively as a verb (*The bank lends him the downpayment*).

less. See **fewer.**

lie, lay. **Lie** (past tense **lay**, past participle **lain**) is an intransitive verb meaning "to rest," "to recline" (*The book lies on the table. It has lain there for three days*). **Lay** (past tense **laid**, past participle **laid**) is a transitive verb (i.e. must be followed by an object) meaning "to put down" (*She lays the book on the table. Yesterday she laid the book on the mantelpiece*).

like, as. Avoid the use of **like** as a subordinating conjunction (*At a party, he behaves like he does in church*). Use **like** exclusively as a preposition (*At a party, he behaves like a prude*). **As** is the appropriate subordinating conjunction with clauses (*At a party, he behaves as he does in church*).

literally. Originally, **literally** was used as an adverb meaning the opposite of **figuratively.** In recent years, some people have been using the word as an intensifier (*She literally blew her top*). Careful writers still use the word in its original sense of "actually" (*The mother literally washed out her son's mouth with soap*).

loose, lose. These words look alike but do not sound alike. Here is a device to help you remember the difference in meaning. The two *o*'s in **loose** are like two marbles dumped

The Little English Handbook

out of a can (*The dog broke its leash and ran loose in the backyard*). The word **lose** has lost one of its *o*'s (*I always lose my wallet when I go to a carnival*). If these memorizing devices do not help you keep the two words straight, invent your own device.

past, passed. These words are more sound-alikes than look-alikes. The word with the *-ed* is the only one that can be used as a verb (*His car passed mine on the freeway*). The word **past** is versatile: it can be used as a noun (*I recalled my sordid past*), as an adjective (*I recalled the past events*), and as a preposition (*His car sped past mine like a bullet*), but it is never used as a verb.

principal, principle. These words sound alike, but they are spelled differently, and they have different meanings. Whether used as a noun or as an adjective, **principal** carries the meaning of "chief." The chief of a high school is the **principal**. The adjective that means "chief" is always *principal (The principal is the principal administrative officer of a high school)*. The word **principle** is used only as a noun and means "rule," "law" *(A manufacturer shouldn't ignore the basic principles of physics)*.

quote(s). In formal contexts, use **quotation(s)** instead of the colloquial contraction **quote(s).**

reason is because. This phrasing constitutes an example of faulty predication (see section **21**). Write "the reason is that . . ."

reason why. This phrasing is redundant. Instead of writing "The reason why I am unhappy is that I lost my wallet," drop the redundant **why** and write "The reason I am unhappy is that I lost my wallet."

respectfully, respectively. Choose the correct adverb for what you want to say. **Respectfully** means "with respect" (*She answered her mother respectfully*). **Respectively** means "the previously mentioned items in the order in which they are listed" (*Mary Sarton, Emily Doan, and Sarah Fowler were the first, second, and third presidents of the Guild, respectively*).

should of. See **could of**.

so, such. Void the use of **so** or **such** as an unqualified intensifier, as in sentences like "She was so happy," "It was such a cold day." If you must use an intensifier, use such adverbs as **very, exceedingly, unusually** (*She was very happy. It was an unusually cold day*). If you use **so** or **such** to modify an adjective, your readers have a right to expect you to complete the structure with a *that*-clause of result (*She was so happy that she clapped her hands for joy. It was so cold that we clapped our hands to keep warm*).

sort of. See **kind of**.

supposed to, used to. Because it is difficult to hear the -*d* when these phrases are spoken, writers sometimes write "He was suppose to come yesterday. He use to come at noon." Always add the -*d* to these words.

their, there, they're. All three words are pronounced alike. The wrong one is chosen in a particular instance, not because the writer does not know better but because the writer has been careless or inattentive. There [their? they're?] is no need to review the different meanings of these very common words.

The Little English Handbook

try and. In the spoken medium, one frequently hears utterances like "Try and stay within the white lines if you can." Purists still insist that we write "Try to stay within the white lines if you can." So if we want to be "proper," we should always write **try to** instead of **try and**.

used to. See **supposed to**.

where. In colloquial English **that** is frequently substituted for **where** *(I read in the local paper where many crimes are unsolved)*. More formal usage would employ the word **that** *(I read in the local paper that many crimes are unsolved)*.

whose, who's. Since the two words are pronounced alike, it is understandable that writers sometimes make the wrong choice. The word spelled with the apostrophe is the contraction of "who is" *(Who's the principal actor? Who's playing the lead role?)* **Whose** is (1) the interrogative pronoun *(Whose hat is this?)*, (2) the possessive case of the relative pronoun **who** *(John is the man whose son died last week)*.

would of. See **could of**.

Glossary of Grammatical Terms

Some of these terms are defined in the section where they figure prominently. But since many of these terms also occur in other sections where they are not defined, this glossary is provided for the convenience of the curious but puzzled reader.

active verb. See **passive verb.**

adjective clause. An adjective clause is a dependent clause that modifies a noun or a pronoun, much as a simple adjective does.

The relative pronouns **who, which,** and **that** often appear at the head of the adjective clause, serving as the connecting link between the modified noun or pronoun and the clause, which then follows.

The car, **which was old and battered,** served us well.

Those are the houses **that I love best.**

Sometimes the relative pronoun is unexpressed but understood:

The book **I was reading** held my attention. (Here **that** is understood: The book **that** I was reading.)

See **dependent clause, relative pronoun, restrictive adjective clause, non-restrictive adjective clause, modifier.**

adverb clause. An adverb clause is a dependent clause that modifies a verb or verbal, much as a simple adverb does.

The Little English Handbook

The subordinating conjunction (**when, because, so that,** etc.), which appears at the head of the clause, links the adverb clause to the word that it modifies.

When I was ready, I took the examination.

I took the examination **because I was ready.**

To take an examination **when you are not ready** is dangerous.

(Here the adverb clause modifies the infinitive **to take.**)

See **dependent clause, subordinating conjunction, verbal, modifier.**

antecedent. An antecedent is the noun that a pronoun refers to or "stands for."

In the previous sentence, for example, the antecedent of the relative pronoun **that** is **noun.** In the sentence "The mother told her son that his check had arrived," **mother** is the antecedent of the pronoun **her,** and **son** is the antecedent of the pronoun **his.**

See **relative pronoun.**

auxiliary verbs. Auxiliary verbs are those function words— "helping" words (hence, "auxiliary")—that accompany other verb forms to indicate tense or mood or voice.

The following words in boldface are auxiliary verbs:

He **will** walk to work. He **is** walking to work. He **has** walked to work.

He **has been** walking to work. He **could** walk to work. He **must** walk to work.

He **was** driven to work.

See **function words, mood, voice.**

collective noun. A collective noun is a noun that designates a group or class of individuals—e.g., **committee, family, jury, army, faculty** (of a university), **team, crew.**

See **summary noun.**

Glossary of Grammatical Terms

comma splice.   A comma splice is the use of a comma, instead of a co-ordinating conjunction or a semicolon, between the two independent clauses of a compound sentence.

> **X** He could not tolerate noise, noise made him nervous and irritable.

Since the comma is a separating device rather than a joining device, it must be accompanied in this sentence by a co-ordinating conjunction (here **for**), or it must be replaced with a semicolon.

> See **independent clause, compound sentence,** and **co-ordinating conjunction.**

complement.   A complement is the word or phrase, following a verb, that "completes" the predicate of a clause.

A complement may be (1) the object of a transitive verb (He hit **the ball**); (2) the noun or noun phrase following the verb **to be** (he is **an honours student**); or (3) the adjective following the verb **to be** or a linking verb (He is **happy.** The milk tastes **sour**.).

> See **transitive verb, linking verb, to be, predicate complement,** and **noun phrase.**

complex sentence.   A complex sentence is one that consists of one independent clause and one or more dependent clauses.

The following complex sentence has two dependent clauses—the first one an adverb clause, the second an adjective clause:

> **When he got to the microphone,** he made a proposal **that won unanimous approval.**

As used by grammarians, the term has nothing to do with the length or complexity of the sentence.

> See **independent clause** and **dependent clause.**

The Little English Handbook

compound sentence.   A compound sentence is one that
consists of two or more independent clauses.

> He was twenty-one, but she was only eighteen.
> Young men are idealists; old men are realists.

See **independent clause** and **comma splice.**

compound word.   A compound word is a combination of
two or more words functioning as a single word.

There are compounds that function as a noun (a **stand-
in**), as an adjective (**eighteenth-century** literature), as a
verb (they **pistol-whipped** him), or as an adverb (he had
to comply **willy-nilly**). Some compounds have been used
so often that they are written out with no space and no
hyphen between the component parts (e.g., **handbook,
skyscraper**). Other compounds, especially those used
as adjectives, are written with a hyphen (e.g., his **never-
say-die** attitude). When in doubt about whether a compound should be hyphenated, consult a dictionary.

co-ordinate.   Words, phrases, and clauses of the same
grammatical kind or of equal rank are said to be "co-
ordinate."

A pair or series of nouns, for instance, would be a co-
ordinate unit. An infinitive phrase yoked with a participial
phrase would not be a co-ordinate unit, because the
phrases are not of the same grammatical kind. An independent clause would not be co-ordinate with a dependent or subordinate clause, because the two clauses
are not of equal rank. An alternative term for **co-ordinate**
is **parallel.**

See **parallelism** and **co-ordinating conjunction.**

co-ordinating conjunction.   A co-ordinating conjunction
is a word that joins words, phrases, or clauses of the

same kind or rank. It joins nouns with nouns, verbs with verbs, prepositional phrases with prepositional phrases, independent clauses with independent clauses, adverb clauses with adverb clauses, etc.

A co-ordinating conjunction cannot be used to join a noun with an adjective, a prepositional phrase with a gerund phrase, or an independent clause with a dependent clause.

The co-ordinating conjunctions are **and, but, or, for, nor, yet, so.**

See **co-ordinate, correlative conjunctions,** and **subordinating conjunction.**

correlative conjunctions.   Correlative conjunctions are co-ordinating conjunctions that operate in pairs to join co-ordinate structures in a sentence.

The common correlative conjunctions are **either . . . or, neither . . . nor, both . . . and, not only . . . but also,** and **whether . . . or.**

By this act, he renounced **both** his citizenship **and** his civil rights.

See **co-ordinate** and **co-ordinating conjunction.**

dangling verbal.   A dangling verbal is a participle, gerund, or infinitive (or a phrase formed with one of these verbals) that is either unattached to a noun or pronoun or attached to the wrong noun or pronoun.

X Raising his glass, a toast was proposed to the newlyweds by the bride's father.

In this sentence, the participial phrase **raising his glass** is attached to the wrong noun **(toast)** and therefore is said to be "dangling" (it was not the **toast** that was doing the **raising**). The participial phrase will be properly attached if the noun **father** is made the subject of the sentence:

See **verbal** and **verbal phrase.**

demonstrative adjective.   A demonstrative adjective is an adjective that "points to" its noun.

The singular forms are **this** (for closer objects—**this** book) and **that** (for more distant objects—**that** book); the plural forms are **these** and **those.**

dependent clause.   A dependent clause is a group of words that has a subject and a finite verb but that is made part of, or dependent on, a larger structure by a relative pronoun **(who, which, that)** or by a subordinating conjunction **(when, if, because, although,** etc.).

There are three kinds of dependent clause: adjective clause, adverb clause, and noun clause.

A dependent clause cannot stand by itself; it must be joined to an independent clause to make it part of a complete sentence. A dependent clause written with an initial capital letter and with a period or question mark at the end of it is one of the structures that are called *sentence fragments*. An alternative term for **dependent clause** is **subordinate clause.**

See **independent clause, finite verb, adjective clause, adverb clause, noun clause, subordinating conjunction.**

faulty predication.   A faulty predication occurs when the verb or verb phrase of a clause does not fit semantically or syntactically with the subject or noun phrase of the clause. It results from the choice of incompatible words or structures.

X The shortage of funds **claimed** more money.

Glossary of Grammatical Terms

X The reason I couldn't go **was because I hadn't completed my homework.**

The verb **claimed** in the first sentence is semantically incompatible with the noun phrase **the shortage of funds** that serves as the subject of the clause. In the second sentence, the adverbial **because** clause is syntactically incompatible as a predicate complement following the verb **was.**

See **predicate complement, predicate verb, noun phrase, verb phrase.**

finite verb. A finite verb is a verb that is fixed or limited, by its form, in person, number, and tense.

In the sentence "The boy runs to school," the verb **runs** is fixed by its form in person (cf. **I run, you run**), in number (cf. **they run**), and in tense (cf. **he ran**). The verbals (participle, gerund, infinitive) are considered **infinite verbs** because although they are fixed by their form in regard to tense (present or past), they are not limited in person or number. The minimal units of a clause, whether it is dependent or independent, are a subject (a noun phrase) and a finite verb:

Bells ring. (but not: Bells ringing)

See **predicate verb, noun phrase, verbal.**

function words. Function words are those "little words" in the language that have very little vocabulary meaning but that perform such vital functions as connecting or relating other words in the sentence.

Sometimes called *particles,* function words comprise all such words in the language as the following:

(1) articles or determiners (in front of nouns): **the, a, an, this, that, these, those, all, some,** etc.

(2) prepositions (for connecting or relating their objects to some other word in the sentence): **of, from, above, on, at,** etc.

(3) co-ordinating conjunctions (for joining words, phrases, and clauses of equal rank): **and, but, or, for, nor, yet, so.**

(4) subordinating conjunctions (for joining clauses of unequal rank): **when, if, although, because, that,** etc.

(5) auxiliary verbs (for indicating changes in tense and mood): **will, shall, have, may, can, would, should,** etc.

(6) conjunctive adverbs (for providing logical links between clauses): **however, nevertheless, moreover, therefore,** etc.

(7) **not** with **do** or **does** or **did** (for negating a verb):

He **does not** love his mother.

He **did not** love his mother.

fused sentence.   A fused sentence is the joining of two or more independent clauses without any punctuation or co-ordinating conjunction between them.

> **X** He could not believe his eyes mangled bodies were strewn all over the highway.

A fused sentence is also called a **run-on sentence** or a **run-together sentence.**

See **independent clause** and **comma splice.**

genitive case.   The genitive case, a term derived from Latin grammar, is the case formed in English by adding **'s** (to nouns not ending in s), by adding **'** (to nouns ending in s), or by using the preposition **of** followed by a noun or pronoun. Some pronouns also form the genitive case by adding **'s** (e.g., **someone's**).

Glossary of Grammatical Terms

The most common use of the genitive case is to indicate possession: the **boy's** book, the arm **of the boy.**

Some of the other uses of the genitive case are as follows:

genitive of origin: **Beethoven's** symphonies.

subjective genitive: the **king's** murder (ie., the murder that the king committed)

objective genitive: the **king's** murder, the murder **of the king** (i.e., the king as the victim of a murder)

genitive of composition: a ring **of gold**

partitive genitive: a piece **of cheese**

The personal pronouns form the genitive case by a special spelling: **my, his, her, its, your, our, their.**

The genitive formed by adding **'s** or ' to nouns is often called the **possessive case**.

gerund. A gerund is a word that is formed from a verb but that functions as a noun.

Because of its hybrid nature as part verb and part noun, a gerund may take an object, may be modified by an adverb, and may serve in the sentence in any function that a noun can perform. Since, like the present participle, it is formed by adding **-ing** to the base verb, one can distinguish the gerund from the participle by noting whether it functions in the sentence as a noun rather than as an adjective. The following are examples of the gerund or gerund phrase performing various functions of the noun: As subject of the sentence: **Hiking** is his favourite exercise. As object of a verb: He favoured **raising the funds by subscription.**

As complement of the verb **to be:** His most difficult task was **reading all the fine print.**

The Little English Handbook

As object of the preposition: After **reading the book,** he took the examination.
See **verbal phrase** and **dangling verbal.**

independent clause. An independent clause is a group of words that has a subject and a finite verb and that is not made part of a larger structure by a relative pronoun or a subordinating conjunction.

The following group of words is an independent clause because it has a subject and a finite verb:

The **boys tossed** the ball.

The following group of words has the same subject and finite verb, but it is not an independent clause because it is made part of a larger structure by the subordinating conjunction **when:**

X When the boys tossed the ball.

The **when** turns the clause into an adverb clause and thereby makes it part of a larger structure—a sentence consisting of a dependent clause (the adverb clause) and an independent clause (which must be supplied here to make a complete sentence).

See **dependent clause, finite verb, subordinating conjunction,** and **relative pronoun.**

infinitive. An infinitive is a word that is formed from a verb but that functions in the sentence as a noun or as an adjective or as an adverb.

Capable of functioning in these ways, the infinitive is more versatile than the participle, which functions only as an adjective, or the gerund, which functions only as a noun. The infinitive is formed by putting **to** in front of the base verb.

Glossary of Grammatical Terms

Here are some examples of the infinitive or infinitive phrase in its various functions:

As noun (subject of sentence): **To err** is human; **to forgive** is divine.

As adjective (modifying a noun—in this case, **place**): He wanted a place **to store his furniture**

As adverb (modifying a verb—in this case, **waved**): He waved a handkerchief **to gain her attention.**

The following infinitive phrase would be considered a dangling verbal:

X To prevent infection, the finger should be thoroughly washed.

(Corrected: To prevent infection, you should wash the finger thoroughly.)

See **verbal phrase** and **dangling verbal.**

inflection. The inflection of a word is the change of form that it undergoes to show grammatical relation in its context or to express modification of its meaning.

The inflection of the verb *to be* appears in the entry **to be** below.

intransitive verb. An intransitive verb is a verb that expresses action but that does not take an object.

Intransitive verbs cannot be turned into the passive voice. Most action verbs in English have both transitive and intransitive uses, like **I ran swiftly** (intransitive) and **I ran the streetcar** (transitive). But some verbs can be used only transitively, like the verb *to emit,* and some verbs can be used only intransitively, like the verb *to go.* If in doubt about whether a particular verb can be used both transitively and intransitively, consult a dictionary.

The Little English Handbook

The following verbs are all used intransitively:

He **swam** effortlessly.
They **slept** for twelve hours.
She **quarrelled** with her neighbours.

See **transitive verb, passive verb,** and **voice.**

juncture.   Juncture is a grammatical feature only of the spoken language. It concerns the ways in which we divide and articulate the stream of sound to make it intelligible to native speakers of the language.

There is the kind of juncture that operates within and between words to help us discriminate between spoken phrases like "ice cream" and "I scream" or between "great rain" and "gray train." Another group of junctures makes use of various kinds of pauses or lengthening out of syllables to mark off the boundaries and terminations of utterances. This latter kind of juncture is roughly related to the punctuation system—commas, semicolons, periods, and question marks—of the written language.

linking verb.   Linking verbs are those verbs of the senses like **feel, look, smell, taste, sound,** and a limited number of other verbs like **seem, remain, become, appear,** that "link" the subject of the sentence with a complement.

Linking verbs are followed by an adjective or a noun or a noun phrase:

The sweater **felt** soft. (adjective as complement)
He **appeared** calm. (adjective as complement)
He **remains** the president of the union (noun phrase as complement)

See **to be, complement, predicate complement,** and **noun phrase.**

Glossary of Grammatical Terms

modifier.   A modifier is a word, phrase, or clause that limits, specifies, qualifies, or describes another word.

In the phrase "the red barn," the adjectival modifier **red** helps to specify or describe the particular barn being talked about. In the phrase "ran swiftly," the adverbial modifier **swiftly** describes the manner in which the action designated in the verb **ran** was done. Phrases and clauses also modify nouns and verbs:

the girl **with the flowery hat** (prepositional phrase modifying **girl**)
the barn **that is painted red** (adjective clause modifying **barn**)
he ran **down the street** (prepositional phrase modifying ran)
he ran **because he was frightened** (adverb clause modifying **ran**)

Besides modifying verbs, adverbs also modify adjectives and other adverbs:

It was an **unusually** brilliant colour. (modifying the adjective **brilliant**)
He ran **very** swiftly. (modifying the adverb **swiftly**)

See adjective clause, adverb clause, and **squinting modifier.**

mood.   Mood is that aspect of a verb which indicates the speaker's attitude toward the expressed action or condition. The **indicative mood** is used for statements of fact (The report **is** true); the **imperative mood** is used for commands (**Be** still!); the **subjunctive mood** is used to indicate hope or desire (I pray that they **be** happy), possibility (If it **be** true . . .), or condition (If he **were** here . . .). Except for the verb **to be,** the subjective forms of verbs are identical with the indicative forms except in the third-person singular of the present tense—e.g., **if he go** instead of **if he goes.**

The Little English Handbook

nominative case.   The nominative case is the form that a noun or pronoun must take when it appears as the subject of a clause or as the complement of a linking verb or of the verb **to be.**

In modern English, however, a writer has to be concerned about the nominative form only of some pronouns, because now nouns change their form only in the possessive case **(boy's, boys')** and in the plural **(boy, boys; man, men).** The personal pronouns, however, and the relative pronoun **who** are still inflected (e.g., **he, his, him; who, whose, whom**). The nominative case of the personal pronouns are as follows: **I, you, he, she, it, we, they.**

The wrong case (the objective or accusative case) of the pronoun is used in this sentence:

X Me hate the smell of burning rubber.

See **complement** and **inflection.**

non-restrictive adjective clause.   A non-restrictive adjective clause is an adjective clause that supplies information about the noun or pronoun that it modifies but information that is not needed to identify or specify the particular noun or pronoun being talked about.

My father, **who is a college graduate,** cannot get a job.

In this sentence, the adjective clause **who is a college graduate** supplies information about the father, but that information is not needed to identify which father is being talked about. The particular father being talked about is sufficiently identified by the **my.**

A non-restrictive adjective clause must be separated with a comma from the noun or pronoun that it modifies.

See **adjective clause, restrictive adjective clause,** and **modifier.**

noun clause. A noun clause is a dependent clause that can serve almost every function that a noun or pronoun or noun phrase can serve: as subject of the sentence, as an appositive to a noun, as the complement for a verb, as object of a preposition, but not as an indirect object.

The subordinating conjunctions that most often introduce a noun clause are **that** and **whether**—although **that** is sometimes omitted when the noun clause serves as the object of a transitive verb.

That he would make the grade was evident to everyone. (subject of sentence)

He said **he would come.** (object of verb; **that** is omitted here, but it is just as correct to say **that he would come**)

The fact **that I had been sick** did not influence their decision. (in apposition to **fact**)

They asked me about **whether I had seen him recently.** (object of the preposition **about**)

See **dependent clause, noun phrase,** and **complement.**

noun phrase. A noun phrase consists of a noun or a pronoun and all of its modifiers (if any).

In the following sentence all of the words in boldface would be considered part of the noun phrase, which is dominated by the noun **house:**

The big, rambling, clapboard house on the hill belongs to Mrs. Adams.

See **verb phrase** and **verbal phrase.**

parallelism. Parallelism is the grammatical principle according to which words, phrases, or clauses joined in a pair or in a series must be of the same kind.

Nouns must be coupled with nouns; prepositional phrases must be coupled with prepositional phrases; adjective clauses must be coupled with adjective clauses.

Parallelism breaks down, for instance, when a noun is linked with an adjective or a prepositional phrase is linked with a participial phrase. Parallelism has been preserved in the following sentence, because all the words in the series that serves as the predicate complement of the verb **was** are adjectives:

The engine was **compact, durable,** and **efficient.**

See co-ordinate and **co-ordinating conjunction.**

participle.　A participle is a word that is formed from a verb but that functions as an adjective.

Because of its hybrid nature as part verb and part adjective, a participle may take an object, may be modified by an adverb, and may modify a noun or a pronoun.

Pulling his gun quickly from his holster, the sheriff fired a shot before the burglar could jump him.

In that sentence, the participle **pulling** takes an object **(gun)**, is modified by the adverb **quickly** and by the prepositional phrase **from his holster**, and modifies the noun **sheriff.**

The **present participle** is formed by adding **-ing** to the base verb: **pulling, jumping, being.**

The **past participle** is formed by adding **-ed** or **-en** to the base verb or by a special spelling: **pulled, beaten, left, bought.**

The perfect participle is formed with **having** plus the past participle form: **having pulled, having beaten, having left.**

Glossary of Grammatical Terms

The **passive participle** is formed with **having** plus **been** plus the past participle form: **having been pulled, having been beaten, having been left.**
See **verbal phrase** and **dangling verbal.**

passive verb. A passive verb is the form that a predicate verb takes when we want to indicate that the subject of the sentence is the receiver, not the doer, of the action.

The form that we use when we want to indicate that the subject is the doer of the action is called the **active verb.**

Only transitive verbs can be turned into the passive form. The passive verb is made by using some form of the verb **to be** (e.g., **am, is, are, was, were, has been**) and the past participle of the base verb.

The shepherds **tend** the sheep. (active verb)

The sheep **are tended** by the shepherds. (passive verb)

See **predicate verb, transitive verb, past participle, to be.**

possessive case. See **genitive case.**

predicate complement. Some grammarians use the term **predicate complement** to refer to any noun, pronoun, or adjective that follows, or "completes," the verb, whether it be a transitive verb, a linking verb, or the verb **to be.** Other grammarians use the term **object** for the noun or pronoun that follows a transitive verb and reserve the term **predicate complement** for the noun, pronoun, or adjective that follows a linking verb or the verb **to be.**

He is the **president.** (noun following the verb **to be**)

She became the **breadwinner.** (noun following the linking verb)

The pie tastes **good.** (adjective following the linking verb)

See **complement, transitive verb, linking verb, to be.**

The Little English Handbook

predicate verb.   A predicate verb is the finite-verb part of the verb phrase that constitutes the whole predicate of a dependent or independent clause.

In the following sentence, the word in boldface is the predicate verb of the independent clause:

The man **guided** the dogsled through the blinding snowstorm.

See **finite verb** and **verb phrase.**

relative pronoun.   The relative pronouns **who, which, that** serve a grammatical function in an adjective clause (as subject of the clause, as object or predicate complement of the verb of the clause, as object of a preposition in the clause) and also as the connecting link between the adjective clause and the noun or pronoun that the clause modifies.

Who is the only one of these relative pronouns that is inflected: **who** (nominative case), **whose** (possessive case), **whom** (objective case).

See **dependent clause, adjective clause,** and **antecedent.**

restrictive adjective clause.   A restrictive adjective clause is an adjective clause that identifies or specifies the noun or pronoun that it modifies, that "restricts" the meaning to a particular person, place, thing, or idea.

Baseball players who are under contract to a duly franchised professional team are eligible for a pension.

In this sentence, the adjective clause **who are under contract to . . . team** specifies those baseball players who are eligible for a pension. If that adjective clause were enclosed with commas (that is, if it were a **nonrestrictive** clause), the sentence would mean that *all* baseball players are eligible *because* they are under contract to a professional team—a quite different meaning from the sentence that does not have commas enclosing the adjective clause.

A restrictive adjective clause should *not* be separated with a comma from the noun or pronoun that it modifies.

See **adjective clause, non-restrictive clause,** and **modifier.**

run-on sentence.   See **fused sentence.**

sentence fragment.   See **independent clause, dependent clause,** and **finite verb.**

squinting modifier.   A "squinting modifier" is a metaphorical way of referring to an adverb or an adverbial phrase that is placed between two words that it can modify. Because by position it "looks both ways," it results in an ambiguous sentence.

For example: **X** The candidate whom we **favoured enthusiastically** praised our platform.

Since the adverb **enthusiastically** occupies a position between two verbs that it can modify **favoured** and **praised**), we cannot be sure whether it was the favouring or the praising that was done with enthusiasm. Shifting the adverb to a position before **favoured** or after **platform** will relieve the ambiguity.

See **modifier.**

subordinating conjunction.   A subordinating conjunction is a word that serves as the connecting link between an adverb clause or a noun clause and a word in some other structure.

The most common subordinating conjunctions that connect an adverb clause to the verb or verbal that the clause modifies are **when, whenever, because, since, although, though, while, as, after, before, unless, until, in order that, so that.**

The two subordinating conjunctions that serve as the link between the noun clause and another structure are **that** and **whether.** The conjunction **that** is often omitted when the noun clause functions as the object of a verb:

He said [that] the committee would not accept the proposal.

See **co-ordinating conjunction, adverb clause, noun clause.**

summary noun. A summary noun is a word that "sums up" an idea or set of particulars presented in the previous sentence. It is usually accompanied by one of the demonstrative adjectives **this, that, these, those.**

He answered telephones, stuffed envelopes, rang doorbells, collected money, and distributed literature. This **work** [or These **activities**] won him a secure position on the candidate's campaign staff.

To avoid tha vagueness or ambiguity of reference that may result from beginning a sentence with only a **This** or a **These,** the writer should use a summary noun along with **This** or **These** (or **That, Those**).

See **collective noun** and **demonstrative adjective.**

suspended structure. A suspended structure is a phrase whose completion is delayed by an intervening parallel phrase. Both phrases are completed by a common element.

His financial status is related to, and bolstered by, the vigour of the stock market.

Weren't you at all fond of, or in the least bit in sympathy with, my stand on this issue?

Employers are interested in the long-term, as well as the short-term, worth of our graduates.

A comma is usually put at the end of the first arrested phrase in order to signal to the reader that the phrase will be completed later in the sentence. This punctuation represents an exception to the rule stated in **36** that pairs of words, phrases, and dependent clauses joined by one of the co-ordinating conjunctions should not be separated with a comma.

terminal punctuation. Terminal punctuation is the period or question mark placed after a string of words to signal the end of a sentence or utterance.

Commas, semicolons, and colons — sometimes called **internal punctuation** — are used to mark the boundaries of phrases and clauses within the sentence. An alternative term for **terminal punctuation** is **end punctuation.**

to be. **To be** is the infinitive form of the most frequently used verb in the English language, one that can be followed by a noun, a pronoun, an adverb of place (e.g., **there, here, upstairs**), the preposition **like** plus the object of that preposition (e.g., He is **like his father**), a verbal or verbal phrase, or a noun clause.

Here are the various forms of **to be,** as it changes in number, person, and tense: **am, is, are, was, were, shall be, will be, has been, have been, had been, shall have been, will have been.**

Some form of **to be** along with the present participle of the base verb is also used to form the progressive tense of the English verb: He **was going** to the doctor regularly. He **had been going** to the doctor regularly.

Some form of **to be** along with the past participle of the base verb is also used to form a passive verb: He **was struck** on the head. He **has been struck** on the head.

See **linking verb, predicate complement, passive verb,** and **participle.**

The Little English Handbook

transitive verb. A transitive verb is a verb expressing action that terminates in, or is received by, an object.

   The object of a transitive verb can be a noun or noun phrase, a pronoun, a verbal or verbal phrase, or a noun clause.

   They **destroyed** the village. (noun as object)
   They **shot** him. (pronoun as object)
   He **favours** giving me another chance. (gerund phrase as object)
   He **will try** to break the lock. (infinitive phrase as object)
   He **proposed** that everyone in the room be allowed to vote. (noun clause as object)
Only transitive verbs can be turned into passive verbs.
   See **transitive verb** and **passive verb.**

verb phrase. A verb phrase is a group of words consisting of a verb and all of its auxiliaries (if any), all of its complements (if any), and all of its modifiers (if any).

   In the following sentence, all words in boldface would be considered part of the verb phrase (a structure dominated by the verb):

   The army **has been severely restricted in its operations.**
   See **noun phrase, verbal phrase, predicate verb, auxiliary verb, modifier.**

verbal. A verbal is the general name applied to participles, gerunds, and infinitives.

   These words are called "verbals" because they are formed from verbs; because they are not finite verbs, they cannot by themselves serve as the predicate verb of an independent clause or a dependent clause.

   See **participle, gerund, infinitive, finite verb, predicate verb.**

Glossary of Grammatical Terms

verbal phrase.   A verbal phrase is a group of words consisting of a participle or a gerund or an infinitive and all of its complements (if any) and all of its modifiers (if any).

In the following sentence, all words in boldface would be considered part of the verbal phrase, which is dominated by the participle **leaving:**

Leaving behind all of its heavy equipment, the army pressed forward quickly.

voice.   Voice is that aspect of a verb which shows the relation of the subject to the action—that is, whether that of performer or recipient. The former is called **active voice** (I was loving), the latter **passive voice** (I was loved).

See **passive verb.**

Spelling Rules, Examples, Exceptions

Read and understand the Rule	**Study how it is applied in the Examples**	***Learn* the Exceptions**
IE AND *EI*		
1 Put *i* before *e*	→brief, yield, relieve	either, height, seize
2 except after *c*	→receive, conceit ceiling	weird, leisure
UNLESS *c* is pronounced *sh*	→efficient, ancient	
3 and except when the sound is *ay*	→weight, sleigh, their	
ADDING A SUFFIX TO A WORD ENDING IN Y		
1 If *y* is preceded by a vowel, it does not change	→obey/obeyed annoy/annoyance	pay/paid day/daily
2 if *y* is preceded by a consonant, it changes to *i* UNLESS the suffix is *ing*	→heavy/heavier enemy/enemies pity/pitiful →carry/carrying study/studying	shy/shyness dry/dryness
THE FINAL-*E*		
1 Drop the *e* if the suffix begins witth a vowel	→judge/judging advise/advisable sincere/sincerity	Words ending in *ee* or *oe* do not follow this rule: agreeable, canoeing
UNLESS this will cause confusion	→dying/dyeing singing/singeing	
2 Retain the *e* if the suffix begins with a consonant	→manage/management care/careless polite/politeness	true/truly argue/argument

Spelling

DOUBLE FINAL CONSONANTS

1 One-syllable
words double the
final consonant if:
-the word ends in
a *single* consonant
-which is preceded
by a *single* vowel
-and the suffix to
be added begins
with a vowel.

→hit/hitting
run/running
drop/dropping

2 Words of more
than one syllable
follow the pre-
ceding rule if the
accent falls on
the final syllable
of the root word.

→begin/beginning
commit/committee

Accent not falling on
final syllable:
murmur/murmuring
benefit/benefited

SPECIAL CASES

1 -ary, -ery
Most common
words, with few
exceptions, end
in -ary

→*dictionary, secre-*
tary
library, elementary

cemetery, stationery
distillery

2 *able, -ible*
The -able ending
usually occurs if:
-the root word is
complete

→eatable

portable

-the root word
lacks only the
final *e*

→*desir*able

collapsible

-the root word
has had the *y*
changed to *i*

→*reli*able

memorable

The Little English Handbook

UNLESS -*ion can* be added directly to the root word → suggest/suggestion/ suggest*ible* access/accession/ access*ible*

correct/correct*able* detect/detect*able*

3 *Plurals*

-Words ending in an *s* sound (*ss*, *sh*, *z*, *ch*, *x*) add *es* for the plural → business*es*, tax*es*

-Words ending in a *y* preceded by a consonant usually change *y* to *i* and add *es* to form the plural → librar*ies*, arm*ies*

4 Consult a dictionary for words ending in -*ance* and -*ence*. There are no really helpful rules which apply to these words.

Commonly Misspelled Words

accept (cf. except)
accidentally
acquire
acquaintance
address
alright (cf. all right)
already (cf. all ready)
arithmetic
athletics
attendance

believe
benign
business

cemetery
changeable
chief
choose (cf. chose)
conscience
correspondent

definite
dependent
design
devise (cf. device)
diminution
disappearance
dispel

effect (cf. affect)
embarrass
environment
exaggerate
existence

familiar
fascinate
flagrant
foreign
forth (cf. fourth)
fragrant
friend
fulfill *or* fulfil
    (but not *fullfill*)

government

harass
height
hindrance

incredible
independent
irresistible
its (cf. it's)

judgement, judgment

The Little English Handbook

library
lose (cf. loose)

maintenance (cf. maintain)
mathematics
minuscule
miracle
miscellaneous
mischief

necessary
neighbour
noticeable
nuisance

occasion
occurrence
occurred
offered
omitted

parallel
peculiar
possess
preceding (cf. proceeding)
preferred
prejudice
principal (cf. principle)
privilege

quite (cf. quiet)

receive
referring
relieve
remuneration
resemblance
reverence
ridiculous

seize
separate
similar
special
stationary (immobile)
stationery (paper)
succeed

than (cf. then)
their (cf. there)
threshold
too (cf. to)
tragedy
truly

usually

whose (cf. who's)
withhold

CANADIAN VS. AMERICAN SPELLING

Λ number of the words used in this handbook have an alternative American spelling. Since American spelling is gaining popularity in some parts of Canada, we have compiled a list of a few words that have alternative spellings. When you are writing, don't use Canadian spelling for one word and American spelling for another. Choose one method of spelling and stay with it.

CANADIAN	AMERICAN
clamour	clamour
defence	defense
honour	honor
judgement	judgment
labelled	labeled
licence (noun)	license (noun)
license (verb, same)	license (verb, same)
marvellous	marvelous
neighbour	neighbor
practise (verb)	practice (verb)
practice (noun, same)	practice (noun, same)
quarrelled	quarreled
rigour	rigor
rumour	rumor
storey (of building)	story (of building)
theatre	theater
travelled	traveled
vigour	vigor

Some Everyday Metric Units

Quantity	Unit	Symbol
length	millimetre (one thousandth of a metre)	mm
	centimetre (one hundredth of a metre)	cm
	metre	m
	kilometre (one thousand metres)	km
area	square centimetre	cm²
	square metre	m²
	hectare (ten thousand square metres)	ha
volume and capacity	cubic centimetre	cm³
	cubic metre	m³
	millilitre (one thousandth of a litre)	mL
	centilitre (one hundredth of a litre)	cL
	litre	L
mass	gram (one thousandth of a kilogram)	g
	kilogram	kg
	tonne (one thousand kilograms)	t
time	second	s
	minute	min
	hour	h

speed	metres per second	m/s
	kilometres per hour	km/h
temperature	degree Celsius	°C
pressure	pascal	Pa
	kilopascals (one thousand pascals)	kPa

CREDITS

Steinbeck excerpt on page 37.
From THE GRAPES OF WRATH by John Steinbeck
Copyright 1939, © renewed 1967 by John Steinbeck
Reprinted by permission of Viking Penguin Inc.

Index

Index

The Little English Handbook

Index

FORMAT OF MANUSCRIPT

GRAMMAR 8-20 (pp. 5-44)

STYLE 21 -30 (pp. 45-70)

PARAGRAPHING 31-33 (pp. 71-84)

PUNCTUATION 34-45 (pp. 85-112)